This is
GAMBLING

NICK CONSTABLE

Sanctuary

This is
GAMBLING

Printed and bound in Great Britain by Antony Rowe Limited, Chippenham, Wiltshire

Distributed in the US by Publishers Group West

Published by Sanctuary Publishing Limited, Sanctuary House, 45-53 Sinclair Road, London W14 0NS, United Kingdom

www.sanctuarypublishing.com

Cover photograph courtesy of CORBIS

ISBN: 1-86074-495-8

CONTENTS

INTRODUCTION

> 'Life is a gamble at terrible odds – if it was a bet you wouldn't take it.'
>
> – Tom Stoppard, *Rosencrantz And Guildenstern Are Dead*

There's always been a nasty smell around gambling. Not the earthy, pungent whiff of a steaming brown pile in the paddock. That just makes racegoers feel at home. Not the evocative odour of stale sweat, alcohol and tobacco that reminds you you stayed up too late in the poker school. Not even the smell of fries and old carpet that pervades sad, seafront amusement arcades. No, we're talking here about the smell of money. Wads and wads of it. Money that, as my old granny used to say, attracts the 'wrong class of person'.

It's not hard to see why gambling has struggled with its image. Any industry that has been in bed with the Mafia for much of the 20th century can hardly whinge now about being misunderstood. Scams continue to infest sports betting in general and racing in particular to the point that they're viewed by punters as an occupational hazard. Criminals have long used casinos and bookmakers to launder dirty money while stories of addicted gamblers destroying family life are legion. It's not surprising then that politicians have publicly tut-tutted at the whole, dirty betting business while quietly rubbing their hands at the revenue it delivers.

Governments have traditionally handled this hypocrisy by making gambling outlets low key, unattractive and awkward to access. Their role has been that of the muscle-man in a backstreet protection racket. As long as taxes are paid and ground rules are followed then everyone can make a quiet buck. No need to recruit customers because they'll turn up anyway.

This is why America restricts casino gambling to a handful of states and some Indian reservations. It's why Internet bookmakers (who can avoid local taxes) are pursued by US lawyers waving writs. It's why British casinos make you wait 24 hours before your membership is accepted. And its why for years your typical high street bookmaker hid behind darkened windows, as if some terrible plague lurked inside.

For decades these restrictions, and others, have reinforced the dingy image of gambling and played down the fact that it can actually be good fun. The strange thing is, though, everything's about to change. Politicians now see gambling as, officially, a Good Thing. Why the U-turn? As Bill Clinton might say; it's the economy, stupid.

Here's the theory. Encouraging us to bet will generate more tax income, which will mean less bleeding of taxpayers. This will inject more money into the economy, which will improve employment and living standards, and this will result in more popular politicians (see 'World' chapter, p71-2). Leaders of the industrialized nations know that if they're to meet voter demands for better healthcare, schools, transport infrastructure and national security then the usual tax-raising malarkey just won't do. What's needed is a Big Idea to help balance the books. Gambling is it. So welcome to the pleasure dome.

If you need proof that the revolution is upon us then take a look at the UK. Since 1997 the Labour government has carved itself a reputation for being prim and nannyish about health and social issues. Chips are out; fruit and veg are in. Imperial weights are a menace, schoolchildren should do 150 minutes of homework a night, magazines should stop using thin models, TV should stop featuring fat women. You get the drift.

So when in March 2002 Tessa Jowell, Secretary of State for Culture, Media and Sport, was pictured gazing coyly over a roulette table there was a sense of something not being quite right, like discovering your demure, widowed aunt leads a double life in Eminem's backing band. Gambling, with all its addictive baggage and social seediness, suddenly became awfully sexy. It was the latest step in a softening-up process that, according to some commentators, will culminate in glitzy Las Vegas-style casinos along Blackpool seafront.

In fairness the policy shift didn't quite happen overnight. In 2001 the Government's Gambling Review Body, chaired by Sir Alan Budd, published a report suggesting radical ways of modernizing the British gambling industry, increasing turnover and tax-take and effectively setting a new world regulatory standard. Britain has always been seen as a model of betting probity, so whatever it does will steer public policy in other nations – even within the mighty US.

The Secretary of State's croupier pose was a press call to promote the government's official response – a White Paper punnily titled 'A Safe Bet For Success'. Together with the Budd Report this document seems likely to shape the future of gambling around the world. Yet the real driving force has been running for years.

According to Dr Greg Anderson, an economist and administrative director of the Centre for Gambling Studies at Salford University, the re-introduction of a British national lottery in 1994 introduced millions to the idea of regular betting while simultaneously removing the hassle. He says:

It changed the context in which gambling took place. It created the chance to buy lottery tickets for a very modest sum, allowing easy entry into gambling markets. This appealed to those who'd not had gambling opportunities up until then. But it also opened a huge political quandary. How can you have this huge gambling monopoly which is allowed to advertise – albeit in aid of good causes – operating outside a very archaic set of rules for other operators. It was inevitable that the Budd Report would seek to blow away the old restrictions and the government is now clearly on board. Depending on Parliamentary time and commitment, we should see most of the recommendations coming into law over the next few years.

One major effect is likely to be that casinos become a big deal in the UK. Whereas there have never been more than 120 in business up until now, we'll probably see many more small ones and one or two really big operators. No one is quite sure yet how the industry will respond.

So what of Budd's proposals? Essentially, they are geared towards making gambling easier and more profitable – for the industry that is – while toughening up consumer protection, promoting good practice and, allegedly, protecting children and 'vulnerable adults' through a new Gambling Commission. The Commission will enforce a Code of Conduct, presumably naming, shaming and prosecuting any operator that doesn't come up to scratch.

Not everyone is enthusiastic about the new approach. 'Trouble is,' one senior Scotland Yard detective told me, 'the Commission might not have the same powers as we do. At the moment we can seize property relating to gambling investigations and if we find illicit firearms or drugs we can nick people for that too. It's surprising how often these things go together. Will the Commission have the clout?'

Of course, the Budd recommendations are still far from enacted. The only new legislation expected by 2004 is a draft bill to sell off the Tote, the state-run organization that controls pool betting at UK horseracing tracks and operates 400 high-street betting offices. According to *The Sunday Times* the Tote would be worth around £700 million ($1,050 million) on the open market and perhaps £200 million ($300 million) if it were run as a trust. The same article warned that ministers were slowing their gambling reform plans after sports minister Richard Caborn was 'horrified' by Australia's liberal gaming laws during a visit down under.

This may be true, although it's difficult to see how reform can now be avoided. Besides, most of the proposals are not that radical. Sure, we'll see casinos being allowed to advertise and take customers straight off the street. Gambling venues will be permitted, wait for it, to serve alcohol and provide live entertainment. There will be bigger 'rollover' prizes at bingo halls while gambling clubs will be able to offer a wide range of games and unlimited jackpots.

The one really groundbreaking idea is that Britain will administer and regulate online gambling, which will make it the first of the G-8 industrialized countries to do so. The global implications of this are truly awesome because if Internet gambling becomes legal worldwide it will almost certainly drive forward further de-regulation for all forms of gambling.

Incidentally, this book focuses heavily on gambling in western-style economies such as Europe, North America and Australia because that's where the big money is and where the commercial industry has taken root. It's also where the bulk of research on gamblers and gambling addiction has been published. No one is suggesting, for example, that the Chinese don't like a bet. It's just that there are precious few hard facts out East.

If you feel talk of world de-regulation is overblown then consider how fast the British gambling industry has moved with the brakes still on. The latest comprehensive report published by economic analysts KPMG in May 2000 (*The Economic Value And Public Perception Of Gambling In The UK*) puts the nation's gross gambling yield at £7.3 billion ($10.95 billion). This is the amount operators make after winnings are paid but before overheads are deducted. Roughly one-third comes from casinos, bingo halls, slot machines and small lotteries. A little over a third is raked in from the National Lottery and the remainder comes from horseracing, sports and spread betting.

To break this down further, the UK has 122 casinos (more than any other European country apart from France) including 23 in London (more than any other capital city). The annual 'drop' (purchase of gaming chips) is around £3.6 billion ($5.4 billion), of which the casinos retain £619 million ($928.5 million). Together they employ 12,000 people and cater for some 11.8 million separate visits a year by members and guests.

There are 688 commercial bingo clubs with a combined active membership of three million and an estimated total staff of 21,000. These clubs accept total annual stakes of more than £1.1 billion ($1.65 billion). Many also draw a tidy income from the ubiquitous gaming machine, more than 250,000 of which are sited in various 'adult' locations. It is thought a staggering £10 billion ($15 billion) a year is pumped into them, out of which suppliers and site owners collect around £1.6 billion ($2.4 billion). An estimated 21,000 people owe their livelihoods to the slots business. (All figures are taken from the Annual Report Of The Gaming Board For Great Britain 2001/02.)

These statistics suggest that Brits are obsessed by gambling, even without the hard sell. But compared to Americans and Australians the British are tightwad punters. The former spend more than $650 billion (£433 billion) annually – more than they do on food – simply on legal gambling. Add in illegal sports betting, outlawed online gaming and unofficial card schools and the figures become too mind-numbing to be meaningful. As for the Aussies, how is it that a nation of 19 million people can spend £37 billion ($55.5 billion) a year on gambling? This is just £5 billion ($7.5 billion) less than the Brits even though the UK population is three times the size. But enough number crunching for the moment. Winning and losing is about more than filthy lucre.

I should say that this is not a book on how to win, or even how to avoid bankruptcy. It won't explain the secrets of poker or a system for stuffing your bookmaker. Hopefully it will cast some light on the joys and sorrows of gambling, warts and all. Maybe it'll even change your views.

It's also impossible in a book of this size – probably any size – to properly describe the mind games, dramas, strategies, skills and raw nerves that permeate the world's gambling playgrounds. So rather than even try, the first chapter is devoted to a series of cultural snapshots – the British racing tipster, the poker renaissance, American casinos, Australian slots and a pot-pourri of the rest from lotteries to bingo.

Next there's a look at global betting, with an emphasis on the Internet revolution, followed by a bluffer's guide to gambling's long and varied world history. Chapter 4, meanwhile, considers health issues, problem gamblers and the nature of addiction. Finally there's a look at how people make money from this whole dirty business - specifically, dirty money.

But there's only one place to begin a book on gambling and that's under starter's orders.

Ready, jockeys? We're off...

'The race is not always to the swift, nor the battle to the strong – but that's the way to bet.' - Damon Runyon

The finest racehorses may be Arab, the mega prize money is in America but for true race-lovers Britain is gambling's spiritual home. If you've ever strolled across Epsom Downs on Derby day, cheered yourself ragged among the Guinness-fuelled Irish at Cheltenham or heard the rolling thunder of a Grand National field approaching the first at Aintree, then you're probably hooked. But liking horses isn't a prerequisite to liking horseracing. As one cynical newspaper racing correspondent once told me: 'Just study the form. After that all you need to know about horses is that they eat and shit.'

Commercially, the UK racing industry is in sound health. According to the sport's governing body, the British Horseracing Board (BHB), a total of 5.5 million people attended meetings at the country's 59 racecourses in 2002. The total TV audience rose to 400 million and off-course betting for the 2002/03 financial year topped £7.5 billion ($11.25 billion). To service this demand around 14,000 horses are currently in training.

The BHB likes to remind everyone that racing provides two-thirds of the UK betting industry's profits. Even so, a healthy cut is taken by the Horserace Betting Levy Board (£87 million/$130.5 million from off-course bookies in 2002/03) and pumped directly back into the sport's infrastructure. This money might provide improvement grants to racetracks or support for up-and-coming trainers. It certainly helps keep the show on the road. But, as in any symbiotic partnership, the relationship between racing people and betting people can sometimes get a bit hormonal.

Not that this much matters to the millions for whom racing is a true love affair, a passion that unites billionaires and street sweepers. For male devotees (and they usually are male) the idea of being a professional racing gambler is the ultimate dream, on a par with being paid to have sex with beautiful women several times a day. A peek through the door of your friendly neighbourhood bookie will usually reveal why the regulars were right to have chosen gambling over that gigolo career option – whatever their losses. Every day is dress-down Friday and you somehow know you haven't stumbled into a Hugh Grant lookalike contest.

At the other end of the scale there's the toff punter, a beast easily identifiable by its hat style (top in men; unfeasibly large in women). At Epsom or Royal Ascot you won't often find this lot flashing their wads at the cash layers in Tattersalls. Traditionally they deal with the 'rails bookies', so-called because they operate on the railings dividing the members' enclosure from Tattersalls. It's here that most of the on-track credit and high-stakes bets are placed.

> The world's longest-established horserace is said to be the Chester Cup, run at Chester, Cheshire, England. It was first raced in 1511 for the top prize of a silver bell.

In recent years the doyen of the rails men was Dickie Gaskell, 'the gentleman bookie' who sadly died in May 2003 aged 76. Hailing from an old English racing family, Gaskell's networking of the aristocracy was legendary and they came flocking to place wagers with him. As a director of Ladbrokes in the 1960s he was instrumental in building up the business and had a reputation for fearlessness in accepting big bets.

According to one story he took £20,000 ($30,000), which was a massive stake in 1964, from the property developer Bernard Sunley on the 5-1 shot Out and About, running in the '64 Mildmay of Flete Chase at Cheltenham. Out and About was owned by Sunley and he delighted in standing by Gaskell's pitch to give a running commentary on the race. Gaskell remained poker-faced throughout. Sunley lost.

THE RACING TIPSTER

Rich or poor, betting on horses is at best a pleasurable hobby for most of us. Only a highly motivated few will ever make a living out of their bookmaker and then only through exhaustive research, iron willpower and courage – plus a decent wedge of working capital. That initial lump sum is often the hardest bit and it's why Steve Lewis Hamilton bet his house on the horses.

Hamilton's decision to become a professional punter was the greatest gamble of his life. In the early '90s he was working at London's Smithfield Market as a meat porter, supplementing his wages with £10 ($15) bets that netted around £50 ($75) per week. Then a jokey exchange with a relative about what constituted the perfect job made up his mind. A few weeks later he'd secured a £10,000 ($15,000) 'home improvement loan' from an unsuspecting bank manager and he was away...

For the first couple of years Hamilton served a punishing apprenticeship. He hadn't the confidence to throw everything in and gamble full time so he persisted with his Smithfield job, working dawn-to-noon shifts and trekking around racetracks in the afternoon. His reputation on the circuit got him work with another pro-gambler but after two years his betting log suggested he could go solo. He quit his Smithfield job, moved his family north from London to Chesterfield and hit the formbook with a vengeance.

Dissecting a horse's form is a gruelling process. Previous performances have to be checked against variables such as the experience of trainer and jockey, any weight handicap, the ground conditions or 'going', the animal's preferred racetracks and its likely main rivals. Every day the formbook launches Hamilton's quest for the punter's holy grail or 'value bet', namely any horse with a significantly better chance than the odds suggest. He still gets irritated by those who think he shuts his eyes and sticks pins on racecards.

At the end of each day I review my performance. If things have gone badly I can usually see why I've lost and provided I've done nothing wrong in my preparation I can accept it. But if I've had a bad day and I've placed poor bets, that really infuriates me. If you call yourself a professional then you must be professional.

Discipline is the number one factor. To be able not to bet when you've lost. The big temptation for all punters is to chase losses when you're down on the day and I've dropped into that trap myself. You're down, you spot a horse in the last race and you tell yourself it'll get you out of trouble. Never, ever do it. Not if you want to beat the bookie long-term. The right strategy is to walk away and start planning again in the morning.

For the ordinary punter it's important to be selective. Rather than go through every card you should follow a particular type of race. So on the flat you look for either sprints or staying races. Over the jumps follow novice hurdles or novice chases or whatever. At least this way you get to know your horses and the form falls more easily into place.

Of course, there are a thousand tipsters out there offering to do the job for you. Respond to their adverts and you'll drown in a sea of junk mail within ten working days. The deal is that you pay a modest fee and they provide tips, systems and guarantees of varying worth to make you money. Why don't they get rich following their own tips? They'll tell you it's because they're so good bookmakers refuse to take their money. This is true in a few cases but Hamilton – now a respected web tipster himself – believes most operators are either incompetent or useless.

There are a few tipsters who put the work in and I respect their judgement. But the majority are just marketeers trying to entice punters. There's so many come in to the game pretending they can make it pay. Often they use money from other businesses and very few last more than a year or two. Their temperament lets them down.

The website has been good for me but it is an extra pressure. If you put up three or four winners on the trot they think you're Jesus. Put up three or four losers and you're the devil incarnate. Fortunately most of the present members have been with me a long time and they understand my methods. They know you get days where you do everything right and still lose. As long as your strategy is good, you're betting properly, you have the right personality and you don't fall into all the traps you'll be OK long term. There is no system. I analyze each race, price the horses myself individually and where there's value to be had we back 'em.

Hamilton believes the Internet betting exchanges (see p63) have given ordinary punters their best-ever chance to turn pro. 'But you should never put yourself under pressure,' he says. 'If you can't afford to bet and lose, don't bet.

'You need a comfort zone to keep you sane and gambling the rent money is not the way. Build up a betting bank before you start, keep a record of every bet and the result so you know how you're doing. People quickly forget losing bets. Whatever you do you shouldn't follow my lead and take out a bank loan. That really could have gone horribly wrong.'

The view that racing punters have never had it so good is shared by John McCririck, TV presenter for the UK's Channel 4 Racing. McCririck is a gambling legend who began his career as a bookie in the school playground, graduated to the professional ranks, worked as a racecourse tic-tac man (one who uses arm-waving semaphore to exchange betting information), switched to racing journalism and finally redefined eccentricity as a TV pundit. He's also fond of staccato answers ending with the instruction, 'Go on,' as though he's urging you down the home straight at Newmarket. 'The bookies must take serious money to survive because they're in the ultimate free market,' he says. 'If they don't offer the best possible price the punter can simply walk next door.'

He has time for few professional tipsters but ranks his fellow broadcaster Jim McGrath, of Timeform, among the best. 'He has total dedication, persistence and self-discipline,' says McCririck. 'He documents all his bets so you can judge his performance.' Let's just say you do not want to be Jim McGrath's bookmaker:

Generally, though, anyone who sells betting systems needs to answer one common sense question. Why all the advertising and mailshots?

Why not just back the horse? If I had a system I sure as hell wouldn't be working on Channel 4 – you'd find me in Hawaii tapping the day's selections into a laptop computer from my balcony overlooking the beach.

The system sellers say they have to market their plans because the bookies know their information is red hot and won't take their bets. There was a time when this could, theoretically, have been a reasonable excuse. Nowadays there are unlimited ways to bet and countless bookies who'll take your money. It doesn't wash with me.

I'd say there's never been a better time for a dedicated racing fan to make a living from betting. You can get up-to-date information delivered through the Internet and there's a huge range of bookmakers and meetings to choose from. It's a golden age but if you're going to be successful you've got to learn to lose and lose again and shrug it off as part of the game. It takes great self-control.

If you want to try becoming a pro gambler then fine. But racing is about so much more than that. You get an amazing atmosphere everywhere from the bars to the bookies' pitches. There's the smell of the horses, the ritual of the paddock, the tension as start time approaches, the punters scrambling to get their money on, the celebrations or commiserations afterwards. It's a brilliant, exciting day out. And the racetrack is a fantastic place to pull women.

THE POKER RENAISSANCE

Think poker and what do you see? Cowboys, gangsters, punch-ups, shootings, smoke-filled rooms, narrowed eyes, whisky bottles, sweating brows, middle-class intellectuals, TV celebrities?

If you got all but those last two then perhaps you should get out more? Poker is fast becoming the posh person's street cred and the ageing celeb's publicity ticket. It demands skill, balls, an analytical brain and the disciplined facial muscles that only a decent private school education can deliver. It's the misspent youth you never had; the Hollywood fantasy to slaver over and good practice for those tortuous mind games with your partner. Poker is the new sex. And you can do it for hours without popping a single Viagra pill.

Long-standing players must hate the thought of suddenly being trendy. It's a bit like discovering a great band at your local pub and having everyone else catch up just as the spotty youths appear on *Top Of The Pops*. Poker has plenty of working-class pedigree, from barrack rooms to factory canteens; picket lines to pub lock-ins. In the US the game is already so culturally ingrained that there are an estimated 60 million regular players and it's the unofficial subject on every high school curriculum. Now poker's *nouveau* elite is rampant it's only a matter of time before reality TV muscles in with *I'm A Celebrity, Get Me A Poker Game*.

Former World Series poker champion Amarillo Slim was once kidnapped by the henchmen of cocaine baron Pablo Escobar as he promoted a new casino in Colombia. Escobar freed him and later sent an apology – a parcel of uncut emeralds.

The move from smoke-filled cardroom to dinner party chic has been driven by three things. Firstly, cardrooms in Britain are a rare beast. Club managements don't really want them because the space they occupy could be crammed with slot machines churning serious profits. Result – a move towards private games in private homes. Secondly, televised poker tournaments such as the Ladbrokes Poker Million have been a surprise hit in the ratings, sprinkled as they are with pro players and B-list celebs. Viewers perceive the game as a triumph of skill over luck and become instant experts on strategy and analysis. Makes a change from Scrabble perhaps.

Thirdly, poker really is hitting the brainy sector. In 2003 Oxford and Cambridge fought the first ever varsity 'heads-up' team tournament – 12 one-to-one games in which the aim was to wipe out the opponent's chips. The better-known players included the writer and poet Al Alvarez, authors Martin Amis, Salman Rushdie, Tony Holden and Victoria Coren, playwright Patrick Marber and the comic actors Stephen Fry and Ricky Gervais. Alvarez goes so far as to credit poker with transforming his life. His first marriage was disintegrating and he'd attempted suicide when he stumbled by chance on the acclaimed playing manual by Herbert O Yardley *The*

Education Of A Poker Player. The introduction was what most impressed him: 'A card player should learn that once the money is in the pot it isn't his any longer. He should not be influenced by this. He should instead say to himself "Do the odds favour my playing regardless of the money I have already contributed?"'

Alvarez said, 'What was true of money in a card game was equally true of the feelings I had invested in my disastrous personal affairs. Do the odds favour my playing regardless of what I had already contributed. I knew the answer...poker really does teach you to grow up.' (Quoted in the *Daily Telegraph*, 3 March 2001.)

Like all great games the rules are simple, but the winning is hard. Poker comes in dozens of wrappings such as five-card draw, Texas hold-em, Omaha, Omaha hi-lo, seven-card stud and lo-ball. These are all variations of a basic theme in which you are dealt cards (face up or down) and place wagers to stay in the game or draw more cards until hands are revealed.

Starting at the top the hands to look for are the royal flush (a run of cards in the same suit) four-of-a-kind (ie four aces), ordinary run (mixed suits in numerical order), ordinary flush (all the same suit), full house (a pair plus three of a kind), a pair or even a single high card. In tournament play everyone starts with the same number of chips but there are usually limited 're-buys' – adding to the eventual prize money – if you find your pile is diminishing.

With a good hand it's in your interests to keep other players in the game. That means not chucking all your chips into the pot (which they'd need to match) and scaring them into folding. It is much better for them to keep contributing to your winnings! Equally, if you really know what you're doing you might bet half your bankroll on a pair of twos and bluff your way through. There are entire libraries covering strategy and people who devote their every waking hour to studying it. The point is that poker isn't just about holding good cards; it depends on interpreting the tells, the body language and playing style of opponents. This is the game's great intellectual appeal; the 'reading' of other players and the battle to out-think them.

Professionals – and there are very few of those – will advise rank amateurs to follow the KISS (Keep It Simple, Stupid) rule. This means playing tight and folding early. Roughly translated, 'tight' means taking on only the best hands but betting with real aggression. It works on the basis that too many poker hopefuls play too many mediocre hands for too long. Folding early sounds like the same advice but it's not. If you've waited ages for a good hand you feel under pressure to back it. If others around you are also betting heavily this may not be a great idea as they may have an even better hand than you. Serious players pride themselves on a dispassionate ability to fold good cards.

Mark Strahan is a life-long player who now runs Britain's leading poker website, ukpoker.com. He reckons a sound poker theory usually pays dividends but that the golden rule is that there are no golden rules.

I don't care how many books you read. You need cardroom experience. If your entire bankroll is £100 then you're scared shitless of losing £100. Doesn't matter what hand you've got.

Some people say that if your first two cards are a pair of aces you should stick everything in because you've got great cards. Suppose you do that and four people call you. You think great, there's £400 in that pot. In fact your chances of winning have dropped like a stone because you've got yourself four opponents. It's not like you're going head to head.

With care you can control your expense. Crazy games like six-card Omaha are great for gamblers but if you want a decent chance to make money you should stay away from them. I'd advise new players to try Texas hold-em, seven-card stud or maybe four-card Omaha. In any case you should play to your limits. I may be addicted to this game but I'm not looking to win £400,000 on a single hand. For some professionals that kind of money is just a tool of the trade.

He means people like Amarillo Slim - aka Thomas Austin Preston Jr of Amarillo, Texas - who has been cutting it as a pro-gambler for half a century. As a former champion of poker's World Series, Slim's proud boast is that he's won card games with pots 'bigger'n a show dog could jump over'. He reportedly won $1.6 million (£1 million) off girlie-magazine publisher Larry Flynt in a single day and is credited with one of poker's greatest slices of homespun wisdom: 'If you don't see a sucker at the table, it's you.'

Slim's philosophy for winning is simple, which is not the same thing as easy. 'With poker you got to play the people not the cards,' he told the *Daily Telegraph*. 'Remember, you know the hand you're holding. What you have to figure out is what the other guy's got. The secret to that is in the eyes. Don't listen to the guy, don't stare at the table, watch his eyes and learn to read what they tell you. Is he bluffing? What's he holding? Read his eyes.'

Perhaps Slim should do an agony-aunt column for Strahan's website. The message board there bears witness to some classic poker angst, such as that from one contributor calling himself 'Cawt By The Nuts'. He wrote pleading for help after being unable to handle a maniac raiser during tournament play. 'I got involved in several pots with him on the basis that he couldn't be holding good cards every time,' said Cawt. 'But I ended up buying in on far too many occasions and his hand kept winning. I found myself flustered and worrying too much about what he was doing.' The replies pulled no punches. 'Only one thing beats really bad players...good cards,' said one correspondent. 'That's it. If you don't get them you won't win. If you restrict yourself to playing good cards then, when unlucky, you will have at most about three re-buys. Our hero however will often have eight or nine. That's your edge.' The point here is that by playing tight you force a bad player to increase his re-buys and up the prize money.

Strahan wants to see a national card club in Britain, similar to existing models in Europe and America. He reckons there are thousands of serious players and points to the 2000 hits per week logged by his own website. However, the sniffiness of UK casinos towards public poker games led to four cardrooms closing in 2002 (in Reading, Birmingham, Bristol and London). Incredibly, there is now just one dedicated public cardroom serving the capital.

We need venues in big towns and cities where you can go just to play cards. That takes away some of the other elements of gambling. If on a weekend night you go to Hollywood Park in LA – a racetrack to all intents and purposes – you'll find a cardroom with literally 80 tables full of people. Six hundred people playing cards at any one time. You could never imagine that in the UK because it's such a grand scale.

A London card club could easily fill 15 tables a night and the house would take a rake off each pot. There's an interesting concept at the Concord club in Vienna where the dealers pay the club for the privilege of dealing. The dealers are self-employed and they take a rake from each pot. They make a good living and it means the club gets a return on investment.

If you really want to see poker, see the business it can do, go to Binion's in Las Vegas at the end of April for the World Series. It's fantastic. Benny Binion invented the World Series and he recognized that what people want to see is big money. Who's interested in a pile of pennies? But if a million dollars is resting on the turn of a card...now that's interesting.

This is why the Ladbrokes Poker Million tournament has been so successful. The celebrity poker games were fantastic to watch because you had professionals playing amateurs and all the usual rules and strategies went out the window. You got celebs winning because they didn't have a clue what they were doing. You don't need to know a lot to win. You just need to be lucky. Cards is 90 per cent luck and 10 per cent skills, and that's the beauty of the game.

Jimmy White would go along with that. He was one of the sporting celebs thrown in to the mix for Sky TV's coverage of the 2003 UK Poker Million event. Together with fellow snooker player Steve Davis, and Europe's Ryder Cup captain Sam Torrance, White's role was to provide a bit of glitz for the viewers. The three of them were cannon fodder for the big guns – professional players like Joe 'The Elegance' Beevers and Tony 'The Lizard' Bloom.

Only it didn't quite happen like that. While Torrance succumbed in the early stages, both Davis and White won their heats, gobsmacking the poker community in the process. Of these two Davis was considered the better player and he finished fifth, trousering a cool $30,000 (£20,000) in the process. 'I didn't know what I was doing out there,' he said afterwards. 'I've been playing regularly on the Internet...but sitting down with real human beings – professionals – is very different. My head was in a jamjar. I couldn't remember my cards. They might have been blue for all I knew. I was trying to maintain control but I could feel my eye twitching. No point trying to bluff after that. (Taken from *The Observer*, 16 March 2003).

If Davis was hot, White was on fire. Having made it to the final he started the game a 12–1 outsider but his run of good cards saw off a clutch of opponents to leave a final showdown against Beevers. White then secured the $150,000 (£100,000) top prize with a pair of aces, beating Beevers' pair of jacks. He couldn't quite take it in.

'I've been gambling since the age of 12,' he said afterwards. 'Horses, dogs, dice, roulette – you name it. I don't play the other games any more but if I'd been betting on this I'd have backed Joe. It must be ten years since I've won this kind of money in a final. And that was snooker.'

CASINO CULTURE

Poker prize money sounds impressive but it's rarely a game played for *really* high stakes. One reason is that the wealthiest gamblers can't be arsed to run their diaries around other wealthy gamblers for the sake of one-upmanship or intellectual jack-offs at a pre-arranged poker school. Far simpler to pop into a casino and take on the house whenever it suits. And if you're going to play cards against the house, blackjack's your game.

There's more on blackjack (or pontoon as the British call it) in the 'History' chapter (see p104) but suffice to say that if you play with 'perfect basic strategy' then over time you should win back 99 cents of every dollar wagered. That's a tight house edge and easily enough to get the gambling 'whales', or high rollers, interested. How wealthy are they? Well, there's rich, there's very rich and then there's Kerry Packer.

Of all the big money players on the world gambling circuit there's none to match the Australian media tycoon's living legend status. In 1999 the US magazine *Gambling News* suggested that only the Sultan of Brunei and the Saudi arms dealer Adnan Khashoggi were in his league and as neither of them are exactly media tarts it's Packer who tends to dominate the gossip column casino talk. Not all the stories about him are apocryphal...

According to the Packer family history, Kerry owes much to his grandfather who chanced upon a ten shilling note in a Tasmanian street, stuck it on a racehorse and with the winnings paid for passage to the mainland to work as a journalist and establish a publishing dynasty. It's this kind of indifference to luck and money that characterizes Packer's own casino play and arguably his business strategies. With a personal fortune estimated at AUS$3 billion (£1.2 billion) in 2002, he must be doing something right.

Casinos and gamblers are wary of discussing their losses but few within the industry dispute that during the '90s Packer really did take the Las Vegas MGM Grand for $26 million (£17 million) at blackjack, playing six hands at a time for $200,000 (£133,000) a hand. This was enough for one or two nervous casino managers to suggest afterwards that he might like to play elsewhere or else accept a cap on his stake money (a politer way of kicking him out). And yet Packer *does* lose. Big time.

In September 1999 he was widely reported to have unloaded £11 million ($16.5 million) during a losing streak at Crockfords casino in London, dwarfing the previous British record loss of £8 million ($12 million) by the Greek millionaire Frank Sarakakis, also at Crockfords. A year later there were reports of an even bigger reverse – $20 million (£13 million) – playing baccarat at the Bellagio's in Las Vegas, the largest single loss in the city's history.

According to friends such mind-boggling sums matter little to Packer. Tales abound of him lending huge sums to fellow players, such as the actor George Hamilton who borrowed £125,000 ($187,500) in order to split two aces during a pontoon game. Hamilton hit 21 on both but Packer refused to take a penny more than the original loan.

Despite the welcome publicity they generate, celebrity gamblers of Packeresque proportions are not always welcomed by the big casinos. This is because house profits are guaranteed by the laws of odds and average over a long period. If you know that roulette is going to make you two to five cents for every dollar wagered and that keno (a casino version of the lottery) will earn 25 cents a dollar and that millions of people will play slot machines paying out 95 per cent of the take, then you don't need shrewd, wealthy blackjack players to start skewing the maths short term.

> 'One of the greatest Vegas tricks is to make every gambler a King... If you just throw the dice or step into a casino, you're at least a duchess, the customer is immediately ennobled, made a Knight of the Garter, a Chevalier of the Legion of Honour.' Mario Puzo, *Inside Las Vegas*

Vic Taucer, head of the US company Casino Creations and professor of casino management at the University & Community College Systems of Nevada, attests that such caution is intensified by the demands of Wall Street. 'In the US, most casinos are corporate entities,' he observes. 'Corporate executives live or die by the quarterly financial reports and if they have a bad quarter because they got beat up by a big player it doesn't look good for management. This is why some casinos actively deter high rollers. They just lower the stake limit.

'What they want is steady, regular income from steady regular gamblers because there's no risk involved. The odds will always work out eventually. Sure, a manager can go after high rollers, maybe high-level baccarat players, and he could make his casino a lot of money. But there are going to be times when those players win and walk away and that manager is suddenly not a popular guy in the boardroom.'

Figures from commercial casinos in the US bear this out. If managers relied merely on a handful of big-time gamblers they could never return such consistently healthy profits. The best indicator of the industry's performance is the gross gambling revenue (GGR), or the amount of money wagered minus winnings returned to players. The GGR is the equivalent of sales rather than profits and so it excludes a casino's overheads like taxes, salaries and running costs.

According to figures quoted by the American Gaming Association, commercial casino GGR for 2001 stood at $27.2 billion (£18.6 billion). This is the culmination of ten years' growth, clearly shown in the table on the next page:

YEAR	BILLIONS OF DOLLARS
1991	8.6
1992	9.6
1993	11.2
1994	13.8
1995	16.0
1996	17.1
1997	18.2
1998	19.7
1999	22.2
2000	24.3*
2001	27.2

(* *Does not include cruise-ship gambling or certain casino devices. Figures from Christiansen Capital Advisers LLC.*)

In terms of the total amount gambled by Americans – known as the 'handle' – casinos are way out in front. Their handle for 1997 was more than 70 per cent of the total, ahead of Native American gaming (12 per cent) and lotteries (8 per cent). Horses, video lotteries and charitable gaming each claimed a 3 per cent slice. Gambling was the second-biggest US leisure spending activity at just over $50 billion (£33 billion), with only video and audio equipment ($80 billion/£53 billion) more popular. Revenues from films and spectator sports weren't in the same league. Both of these categories came in below $8 billion/£5 billion (figures from *International Gaming & Wagering Business* magazine, August 1998).

Only 11 US states permit commercial casinos, although 28 states allow them in Native American reservations as a way of boosting run-down economies. The Indians secured this dispensation partly because they can genuinely claim gambling as a historic part of their culture. Their ancestors believed gambling games were directed by supernatural forces and that the games could predict or influence real-life events (see p79). During the 1980s the Indians started running bingo halls and, because of the semi-autonomous status accorded them by the Federal Government, they were gradually able to repackage these as casinos. In 1997–98, 185 tribal governments obtained a total annual income of $6 billion (£4 billion) from them.

It isn't the case that the biggest casinos make most money per player. A study in Canada (*The WAGER* newsletter, Harvard Medical School, 21

April 1998) showed that the Casino Niagra grossed $42.3 million (£28 million) from an average daily attendance of 20,500, earning an average of $66.56 (£44.4) per player. Yet the Casino Windsor, which logged just 11,800 players, grossed $41.7 million (£27.8 million) giving it an average take of $114 (£76).

Of the 11 US commercial casino states, South Dakota props up the list with a mere $58.6 million (£39 million) GGR. Working our way up we have Illinois, Indiana and Louisiana in joint fourth on $1.8 billion (£1.2 billion), Mississippi third on $2.7 billion (£1.8 billion) and New Jersey second, raking in an impressive $4.3 billion (£2.86 billion) from its 12 casinos. But right at the top, in its own one-state league, stands Nevada with 247 casinos – more than half the national total – and a GGR of $9.5 billion (£6.3 billion). For Nevada you might as well read Las Vegas, the city that sold its soul to gambling.

GAMBLER'S PARADISE

Enter Las Vegas and you're part of a fantasy world in which the gambler plays Hero and Time is the wicked witch. You won't find clocks in the casinos because they just remind customers how late it's getting. For the same reason windows are a no-no. If players see it getting dark outside they might think it's time for bed. As for 'Exit' signs, forget it. If you're not going to gamble you can just wander round the maze of slots until you collapse against that 'double-bucks-jackpot-stampede' machine.

As a kid I used to have nightmares about being lost in a busy city, screaming for help, begging for a way out and realizing no one cared. I'd stumble into a bizarre-looking building and discover a feeding frenzy taking place at a junket inside. At that time I'd never been to Las Vegas but perhaps I was having a transatlantic out-of-body experience. The real Vegas seems uncomfortably familiar...

If you live in the city centre you'll struggle to find a shop that sells shoelaces or fuses or toothbrushes. But if you fancy a cheap night in a motel, or you want to get married immediately, your daily diet is Coke and M&Ms or you need a bail bond agent, a tattoo, a pawn shop or a spot of lap-dancing action then downtown Vegas is your spiritual home.

The casinos all have different faces. Walk the streets and you'll find the Venetian (supposedly a Venice theme), the New York, New York (New York), Excalibur (King Arthur's England), Luxor (Ancient Egypt) and Caesar's Palace (Ancient Rome). Inside, however, the formula of lights, music and action is interchangeable. Croupiers try not to yawn, tightly clothed waitresses bounce breasts and wiggle ass, security officers look mean and 'lurkers'- middle-aged women with bags of dimes waiting for heavily played slot machines to fall ripe for a payout – haunt the gambling floors. There's a surround-sound of snapping cards from the pits, indistinct top 40 songs and tinkling coins and tokens. There's offers of free food and drink as long as you keep betting. But loud or sudden noises are OUT. Mustn't make the punters jumpy...

Infusing the heady atmosphere is a general air of wealth and luxury, as though to remind everyone what they're doing here. Thousands of metres of rich, geometric deep-pile carpet line the walkways, recessed lighting counteracts the flashing aggression of the slots, and air-conditioning machines squirt oxygen to keep everyone awake and spending. Recently casino owners have been bringing high art into the equation. The Venetian's owner Sheldon Adelson has spent $30 million (£20 million) in order to display works by Picasso, Cézanne and Kandinsky (among others) while in May 2003 the gaming billionaire Steve Wynn shelled out more than $40 million (£27 million) on paintings by Cézanne and Renoir. He plans to display them in his new Le Reve casino, due to open in Vegas during 2005.

Etiquette is naturally all-important. 'Don't whine when ya lose,' one Vegas manager told me, 'and don't start whoopin' when you's winnin'. Don't crowd folks when they's gamblin', don't stand close behind 'em, don't bump into 'em and rub bad luck on 'em. Most important don't go pleadin' to be let in with the whales. If you need to ask how much you got to stake to be playin' with those guys then you ain't rich enough. And if you is rich enough then stay cool 'cause all hell be damned we'll find you!'

The idea that casino managers think about luck – even though they know the maths of gambling better than anyone – is curious. Vic Taucer tells how, as a card dealer in Vegas during the 1970s, his pit boss would regularly change the roster to find the 'lucky dealer' who could beat a winning player. Sometimes a dealer would have to switch his shuffle technique to find the 'lucky' method. Salt would be shaken on unopened packs. Dice would be changed on the craps table. Incredibly, for such a hi-tech, analytical industry, this kind of stuff still goes on but Taucer's formula is as follows:

> *It's a pretty simple thing. The customer makes a bet on the outcome of an event. The casino makes a payoff of an amount less than the probability the event dictates, thus creating a casino advantage. The dealer cranks out a certain amount of gambling decisions per hour.*
>
> *The pit personnel's role is to ensure the formula stays intact. If we do not change the casino's advantage, if we ensure the right amount of decisions per hour and keep chips in the betting circles, the pit makes money. But mathematics is the determinant, not superstition.*

The above formula will always work in the end but nothing can protect a casino against the one-off, slightly crazy gambler. In January 1994 a British roulette novice called Christopher Boyd sold his house, cashed all his savings and flew to Vegas where he persuaded staff at Binion's casino to suspend its usual limit on even money bets – ie red against black or odd against even. Not only that, but Binion's agreed to block off the two green-coloured zeros for one all-or-nothing spin. Put simply, the house's slender advantage on an even money chance is achieved by freezing (known as 'en prison') or claiming bets when a zero comes up.

Boyd was allowed one practice spin and then calmly staked £147,000 (around $220,000) worth of chips on red. Number seven came up and he left the casino with his winnings vowing never to gamble again. 'He had,' said one Binion's manager, 'a lot of style.'

Boyd was a one-off but regular players will, unless they're extraordinarily lucky, always lose eventually. Big-time losers don't all have Kerry Packer's *laissez-faire* attitude and they expect dealers and managers to keep their mouths shut. This applies particularly where the losers are public figures. So when the press manages to expose them you can almost taste the *schadenfreude* in the air. In May 2003 it was William Bennett's turn to be humiliated.

A former White House education secretary and anti-drugs 'tsar' for the Republicans, Bennett had for years been America's moral conscience. He'd sounded off against bleeding heart liberals, promiscuity, drugs, drunkenness and President Bill Clinton's sexual behaviour. So when the magazines *Newsweek* and *Washington Monthly* exposed him as a 'preferred customer' at several Las Vegas and Atlantic City casinos the fallout was predictable. Bennett's claims that he'd 'come out pretty close to even' were ridiculed by the casino sources and it was claimed his losses totalled more than $8 million (£5 million).

Bennett responded with a statement acknowledging that he'd 'done too much gambling' and that it was not an example he wished to set. He told journalists, 'I've gambled all my life and it's never been a moral issue with me. I liked church bingo when I was growing up...I view it as drinking. If you can't handle it, don't do it.' Others weren't so sure. 'Working his way down the list of other people's pleasures, weaknesses and uses of American freedom he just happened to skip over his own,' argued Michael Kinsley in *Slate* magazine. 'How convenient.'

We can't leave casino culture without a final word for Kerry Packer and what many gamblers regard as the greatest betting proposition ever made. According to the story, Packer was sitting in a Las Vegas casino when he noticed a pretty girl clearly unsettled by the attentions of a loud, brash Texan oilman. The Texan kept telling her, and the rest of the table, how amazingly rich he was. Packer leant across.

> 'How much did you say you were worth?'
> '$100 million, sir.'
> 'Tell you what,' said Packer. 'I'll toss you for it.'

PLAYING THE POKIES

Whether or not you believe that story there's no doubting Packer's lovestruck relationship with gambling, a passion shared by millions of his fellow nationals. But actually most Aussies couldn't give a stuff about casinos. Forget the atmosphere, the tension, the eyeballing. Your typical Aussie likes doing it alone; one player against the slot machine. It's gambling's version of masturbation with one important difference – you never want to stop.

The roots of Australia's obsession with slot machines – particularly the 'pokies' beloved by sports clubs – can be found in the History chapter (see pp117). The worry these days is that the phenomenon is unstoppable. Gambling down under has generally increased by 15 per cent since 1997/98 but within this figure the rise in pokie play is extraordinary – 57 per cent in 2002 alone (*Productivity Commission*, 1 January 2003). These are the same jackpot machines that many commentators think will swamp Britain under the gambling reforms mentioned earlier.

Figures published in September 1999 show that Australia has upwards of 184,000 pokies, more than half of them in New South Wales. Together they gobble up some AUS$8 billion (£3.2 billion) every year, although the size of stakes and prizes has dropped from the days when you could risk AUS$100 (£400) to win AUS$10,000 (£4,000). In 2001 the NSW government stepped in with a 'harm minimization' package aimed at reducing jackpots and cutting the speed at which pokies take your money. As a result they no longer accept AUS$50 or $100 bills. Gambling experts argue endlessly about data and research but the one thing on which almost all agree is that pokies are the most pernicious, addictive, insidious form of betting known to humankind. Australia's estimated 300,000 problem gamblers – mostly pokie players – lose an average of AUS$12,000 (£4,782) per year each.

Gabriela Byrne's story is a salutary example. She was addicted to pokies for four years during which time she got through AUS$40,000 (£15,900), two jobs and virtually all her friends. She'd gamble for up to five hours a day, on one occasion spending AUS$1,000 (£398.50) saved for her daughter's school fees. By the end she was contemplating suicide.

'I was vulnerable because I hated my job and I think there was a lack of excitement in my life,' she said. 'After an argument with my boss one day I spent my lunch hour playing them. The flashing lights and risk-taking excited me. I just had an intense urge to feed the machine. But, gradually,

I needed to spend more and more to get the buzz... At one point I remember going into my children's room and thinking that I didn't love them any more – that if they weren't around I could go to the pokies more often' (taken from *The Guardian*, 12 February 2003).

The easy response is simply to label Gabriela as a bad mother. In fact I've heard strikingly similar comments from women who got hooked on cocaine. One aspect of addiction is that it replaces normal feelings, like a computer virus wiping the hard drive of the mind. The fact that a woman can lose arguably her strongest emotion – love for her child – speaks volumes about the psychological forces at work here.

There has been precious little research specifically on women pokie gamblers but one 2000 Australian study, *Females' Coping Styles And Control Over Poker Machine Gambling* (Scannell, Quirk, Smith, Maddern & Dickerson), revealed that levels of gambling control were not related to a woman's age, employment, relationship status or 'life-event stress'. The study of 163 women concluded that those who actively sought professional or social support to tackle gambling problems had higher levels of self-control than those who avoided the issue or simply blamed themselves. Other experts say the evidence doesn't support this conclusion. Roughly translated, the advice from academia to addicted female pokie gamblers is a great big Don't Know.

The science of addiction is indeed horribly uncertain (see 'Health' chapter, p145) but Australia is at least doing *something* to tackle the pokie problem. Up there in the front line is Professor Jan McMillen, a sociologist and director of the Australian National University Centre for Gambling Research in Canberra. In researching this book her name came up very frequently, with plenty of scholarly advice suggesting I 'ask Jan that one'. McMillen, it should be said, also has her critics. But her approach is more common sense than rocket science.

In 1999 the Productivity Commission produced a good report looking at all aspects of gambling in Australia. It noted the industry did not produce the benefits claimed and that there was a social cost. A national survey also showed the overwhelming majority of

Australians – all gamblers – believed things had gone too far, that the pokies did more harm than good. This was the first time we'd ever had a public backlash.

We've needed to be clear about what problem gambling actually is. We don't accept the models that America and most of the UK follow. I used to teach public health and epidemiology, and systems like SOGS [South Oaks Gambling Screen – see page 123], which are supposed to identify people with a disorder, are fundamentally flawed.

The first time I went to an American conference on this there were four of us Aussies sitting in a row. They put up the clinical indicators and we stuck up our hands and shouted 'bingo' to the lot. If we followed the US approach we'd have the entire Australian nation under therapy.

The SOGS model is flawed because it is developed from psychiatric measures. This is not a disease, nor a psychiatric problem. It's not a disorder of individuals. It is a public health issue driven by the industry and you need to look at it as a continuum. Most people who gamble will be at some stage on that continuum in their life.

It's like learning to drive. We all take corners too fast at first but eventually most of us learn to stay on the right side of the road. Because of life's circumstances some people head over a cliff. The Productivity Commission came to the conclusion there is no psychological or psychiatric predisposition which can explain this. It could happen to any of us at any time and that's quite scary.

I take a public health approach. The only way to address problem gambling is through prevention rather than treatment. You still have to help those going over the edge but you must focus on prevention. All the evidence shows that when you get new forms of gambling the problems increase and you get new problems.

McMillen has been working closely with the Queensland government to produce a strategy combining treatment and prevention. It includes advice manuals for every sector of the gambling industry and there are no pulled punches.

Basically, we've got to change the way they run their businesses. We don't know whether it'll work. We're flying blind because no one else has done this. We're using the best knowledge we have plus a little common sense. If you have fast, repetitive games without a break in play then it's going to create problems.

For example, we don't want loyalty programmes encouraging people to spend more on gambling than they can afford. Let's instead give them monthly statements so they know how much their habit is costing. These are very simple things, the sort of consumer protection that exists in other industries such as banking.

I had a visitor from Canada and I took him to a club with 1,100 machines – one of the clubs we'd like to reform. He stared around in wonder saying 'Hey, but there are windows. You've got clocks on the walls.' Of course this is better than North American practices. Better, but not sufficient. The real answer lies in the interface between the player and the machine. So now we're working on breaks in play, slowing machines down, flashing up advice messages and allowing pre-set stake limits.

I'm a gambler and I have a left-pocket-right-pocket strategy. When I go to the track my betting money goes in my left pocket and my winnings go in my right. I never bet out of my right pocket. This is the basic strategy operated by most people who stay on the safe side of the equation. But we do need the industry's support if more people are to take control of their gambling.

One aspect of the pokies that has intrigued Australian researchers is the way men and women adopt different playing strategies. An important study by Nerilee Hing and Helen Breen (*Profiling Lady Luck...* from 2001) interviewed 1,879 Sydney club gamblers who had played slot machines at some time in their life. There was little difference between the sexes as far as problem gambling was concerned (4.1 per cent of the 1,092 men as opposed to 3 per cent of the 787 women) but statistically significant variations as to *how* they gambled.

More women played the two and five cent slots (56.8 per cent as opposed to 44.8 per cent of men) while machines requiring stakes between 10 cents and two dollars were more popular with men (55.2 per cent compared with 43.1 per cent). The authors speculated that women wanted to maximize their gambling time by conserving stake money, perhaps so they could feel part of a community. Just as likely, they didn't want to go home to moaning husbands and screaming kids.

Clearly, there are gambling opportunities that appeal more to women than men. In Britain a survey by Teletext racing in 2001 revealed that female punters betting on the outcome of Channel 4's reality TV show *Big Brother* outnumbered men two to one. But if you really want to see a gambling gender-gap read a paper called *Dogfighting: Symbolic Expression And Validation Of Masculinity* (Evans, Gauthier and Forsyth, 1998), which studies dogfighting in the southern US states of Louisiana and Mississippi. For some reason women don't seem much interested in this 'sport'.

Dogfighting is driven by illegal gambling but, to paraphrase Evans *et al*, it's not so much about winning as it is about proving you're a proper 'dogman'. Dogmen believe that if their animals show 'gameness' it reflects well on their owner's masculinity, aggressiveness, competitiveness and strength. Dogs that die in the ring earn respect; dogs that quit the fight get killed afterwards for being cowards. Anyone for a slice of quiche, boys?

LUCKY NUMBERS

'Maybe, just maybe' and 'It could be you' have been among the sharp advertising slogans that encapsulate the British National Lottery's appeal. Spend a pound and there's a chance you'll win that £10 million ($15 million) rollover jackpot. After all, someone's got to. It's just that the 'maybe' and 'could be' bits aren't terribly clear.

Not surprising, really. Truth is, you've more chance of being struck by lightning 18 times in a given year than you have of correctly selecting six numbers from the lottery pool of 49 in any one draw. For statistics lovers the odds work out something like this:

Dying from drinking detergent ....1 in 23 million
Picking six winning numbers in any one UK
    National Lottery draw...1 in 13.9 million
Getting struck by lightning in a given year ....1 in 750,000
Dying in a job-related accident ....40 in 1 million
Total destruction of the planet by asteroid or meteor in
    the coming year ....1 in 20,000
Being murdered in the coming year ....1 in 11,000

(*Figures:* The WAGER, *Harvard Medical School Division On Addictions, 4 August 1998.*)

So there you have it. Don't lie awake with your lottery ticket under your pillow dreaming of multi-million jackpots because it's 1,272 times *more* likely that sometime over the next 12 months you won't wake up at all owing to Planet Earth being a smoking, blackened hulk of lifeless rock. Far better to follow Pascal's Wager, which suggests you should have a bet on the existence of God. But that's another story (see p87).

If the British National Lottery – now called Lotto – offers a bad deal, spare a thought for America's Powerball punters. The Powerball is a lottery covering 20 US states plus the District of Columbia and you can buy a ticket only in a participating state. Because the densely populated areas of New York and New Jersey are outside this cozy little club, lottery players there head onto Interstate 95 towards Greenwich and the rich, green pastures of Powerball Country, aka Connecticut. They tend to do this in the last few hours before a big jackpot draw.

So when in the summer of 1998 the Powerball pot climbed to a quarter of a billion dollars (yes, you read that right) Interstate 95 became the original Road To Hell. Tens of thousands created gridlock, with the predictable increase in road rage and minor accidents. With no hope of reaching service stations motorists were forced to answer the call of nature as best they could. Let's skip the detail and just say the whole thing ended in a massive political row and an $85,000 (£57,000) overtime bill for Connecticut's Governor. All for a 1 in 80 million chance of winning the Powerball jackpot.

Why, given such appalling odds, do we ever bother? There is a bewildering number of theories on this but psychologist Lola L Lopes's paper, *Between Hope And Fear: The Psychology Of Risk* (1987), offers some clues. She argues that, for natural risk-seekers, the potential advantages of risky action loom far more clearly than any threat to personal security.

In other words there is no analytical assessment between risk and threat because taking the risk is so obviously right. Safe 'n' dull types take the opposite approach, although even they can be swayed when an incomprehensibly high jackpot appeals to their sense of aspiration.

> Since the beginning of the UK National Lottery, calls to Gamblers Anonymous have increased by 17 per cent, though not all were lottery-related.

Other psychologists, such as John Bassili at the University of Toronto, believe mind-numbingly high figures on true odds and probabilities are downplayed by lottery players in the face of powerful media images on winning and spending. Players also see their own ticket as somehow special. 'In the person's mind, the ticket they selected has more value than any other ticket even though the odds are just the same,' he says (*Toronto Star*, 31 July 1998).

In the case of Lotto there are probably other factors at work. The basic £1 stake hardly represents a threat to anyone's security and there's the comforting knowledge that a healthy chunk will be donated to charities and good causes. The addition of scratchcard and online spin-offs has added gambling variety and, as Camelot points out, you have a one in 54 chance of winning some kind of prize, even if it is only a tenner.

According to the National Lottery Commission's annual report for 2001/02, Camelot achieved sales of £4.83 billion ($7.25 billion), a windfall for good causes of £1.52 billion ($2.3 billion), a government rake-off totalling £580 million ($870 million) and prize money of £2.2 billion ($3.3 billion). But remember that old adage about money never buying happiness. Well it certainly hasn't made Camelot's political masters very happy. By the end of 2002 the British culture secretary Tessa Jowell was said to be contemplating re-nationalization of the draw unless the company improved its performance.

On 25 June of the same year there was a revealing little exchange between Camelot's chief executive, Dianne Thompson, and a House of Commons Culture, Media and Sport select committee. Why, the MPs wanted to know, had there been such a slump in ticket sales despite massive promotion of the game's newly launched Lotto brand over the previous two months? Thompson blamed various uncontrollable events, among them the Queen's Golden Jubilee celebrations (two bank holidays' depressed sales) and the English football team's second-round defeat of Denmark during the World Cup ('England playing on a Saturday is bad news for us'). She also cited 'sadly' the Queen Mother's funeral.

Who'd have thought it? The Queen Mum's last act as she departed this mortal coil was to bugger up Camelot's sales figures. And what about the Queen herself, going around shamelessly celebrating 50 years on the throne an' all! As for those bastards Beckham and Owen. Why didn't they just help England crash out in the first round as usual? It's tough enough running a lottery without high-profile saboteurs around.

Thompson went on to defend comments she'd made suggesting lottery players needed to be 'lucky' to win money on the main game. She said many players did not regard £10 ($15) as a win and this was why Camelot had changed the 'It could be you' ad slogan: 'What is happening over time is players fed back [sic] to us, "Well, yes, it probably won't be me."'

Unfortunately the new slogan 'Don't live a little, live a lotto' also proved a flop. It was backed by a £72 million ($108 million) relaunch in which comedian Billy Connolly fronted up ads. These were later voted the most irritating on TV. In fact throughout 2002 and early 2003 the bad news just kept on rolling – a rumoured £12 million ($18 million) loss on special Jubilee jackpot draws, a 5.5 per cent fall in sales for the six months to September 2002 and a reduction in lottery spending from £100 million ($150 million) per week in 1997 to £88 million ($132 million) per week in 2003. This in a year (2002) when overall UK gambling expenditure rose 82 per cent, due largely to the scrapping of betting duty on racing.

Finally, on 28 May 2003, Camelot's annual results showed that National Lottery sales had tumbled from £3.8 billion ($5.7 billion) to below £3.4 billion ($5.1 billion) in the past year, total sales were down by 5.4 per cent to £4.57 billion ($6.85 billion) and money for good causes was down from £1.5 to £1.4 billion. The company's total contract-long sales target of £15 billion ($22.5 billion) now seemed distinctly dreamlike, despite Camelot's insistence that sales of its other games – scratchcards, Thunderball and Lottery Hotpicks – had performed well to achieve a 21 per cent sales rise. The company's chairman, Michael Grade, insisted that 'Camelot's strategy to counter the inevitable sales decline of the mature, main Lotto and return the National Lottery to growth is well advanced.' Hmm.

Professor Ian Walker, an economist at Warwick University, believes Camelot's woes can be traced to the launch of its Wednesday-night draw, in which prize money was 'rolled over' to boost the Saturday jackpot. 'The mistake that they made was that they linked the two together so that Wednesday rolled over into Saturday and Saturday rolled into Wednesday,' he said. 'As a result the Wednesday game is doing very well but the Saturday game has nosedived (from *BBC TV News* 19 May 2003).

Camelot's latest wheeze is to increase still further its stable of games. These will include a European £30 million ($45 million) jackpot draw, combining the British, French and Spanish lotteries, a daily game offering a £30,000 ($45,000) top prize, Lotto on the Internet and a twice-yearly Olympic Mega-Draw designed to raise £750 million ($1,125 million) towards the UK's 2012 Olympic bid.

The company's internal projections show that tickets for the main Lotto draw will fall from 74 per cent of all sales in 2003 to 49 per cent by 2005. But Dianne Thompson says this downturn will be balanced by interest in new games. 'International experience shows that this is the only way to counter falling sales of the main Lotto game and it is a challenge we will tackle with relish,' she said. 'We will benefit from the expansion of our games portfolio and be back in solid growth by next year (*BBC News Online*, 19 May 2003).

Convincing the media will be crucial to this strategy. Right from the start of the lottery in 1994, there has been a love/hate relationship between Camelot and the tabloids. Editors quickly got bored with bog-standard millionaire winners and they were soon poking around for money-can't-buy-happiness stories or, even better, good old-fashioned dirt. Efforts were re-doubled if a winner chose anonymity, a request Camelot was obliged to honour and editors were avowed to circumvent. So when a mystery man scooped the first mega-jackpot – £18 million ($27 million) – in December 1994 the full red-top bandwagon cranked into action.

As a freelance reporter I remember getting a clutch of orders from newsdesks to check out this or that 'suspect', most of whom had been fingered by friends or relatives convinced they knew his identity. The race was finally won by the *News Of The World*, who correctly identified Mukhtar Mohidin, a 42-year-old father of three from Blackburn, Lancashire. Under the tag-line 'His name is Mukhtar. He dreamt of corner shop. Now he's worth £18 million', the paper helpfully offered a potted family history.

But the jewel in its coverage was a full-page picture of Mohidin with his wife Sayeeda, onto which designers had scanned the giant sparkling hand from Camelot's 'It could be you' campaign. The theme of these ads was to show the hand descending, god-like, from the heavens to point at lucky winners. For weeks it dominated TV commercial breaks and prime poster sites. Now the *News Of The World* had it pointing straight at Mukhtar's mugshot. The headline was simple and masterful: 'IT WAS HIM'.

Mohidin's life after that was never quite the same. For one thing many Muslims never forgave him for gambling, a vice forbidden by their religion. Within a year or two his marriage began to crumble and his wife divorced him in 1998. Other big jackpot winners have suffered similar personal setbacks, most notably double glazing salesman Paul Maddison and his business partner Mark Gardiner who won Britain's biggest-ever jackpot of £22,590,829 ($33,886,243) in June 1995. According to the London *Daily Mail* (23 April 2003) Maddison became a recluse in Scotland having walked out on his third wife, while Gardiner was divorced by his third wife shortly after scooping the cash. The two men, it was reported, are 'not on speaking terms'.

Of course, there are plenty of big winners who do get on with enjoying their wealth away from the tabloids' gaze. Lower ticket sales – and therefore jackpots – have also tended to take the heat off. Nowadays if you want some real tension in your number action there's only one place to go. Ready? Eyes down.

NUMBER GAMES

Bingo used to be strictly for coffin-dodgers, a way of passing the time until the Grim Reaper came to call. Not any more. Bingo is now cool, fun and sexy – proved by the fact that celebrities play it. Here's a few big-name dabbers to be going on with: Bianca and Jade Jagger, Elle MacPherson, Catherine Zeta-Jones, Yasmin Le Bon, Denise Van Outen, Emma Bunton, Chris Evans, Bono, Paul Gascoigne (no, really), Sara Cox, Atomic Kitten, Damon Hill and Charlie Dimmock. In the video for his single 'Feel', Robbie Williams takes Daryl Hannah for a game of bingo and a plate of chips – and remember, Robbie's rich beyond his wildest dreams. Oh, and *Gladiator* heart throb Russell Crowe used to be a bingo caller in New Zealand.

In Britain, dabbers (so-called because you 'dab' the numbers on your card with a big, blunt pen) have been revitalized by the scrapping of betting duty and new Sunday-night jackpot games in which bingo halls around the country link up by computer. There's a top prize of £250,000 ($375,000) and the halls claim you are 13 times more likely to win £200,000 ($300,000) on bingo than you are on the lottery. Two-hour sessions usually produce around 20 games with players vying to make the magic call of 'House', which means they have dabbed every number on their card. The old, numbered ping-pong balls retrieved manually by a caller are *soooo* last year. These days the big halls prefer random number generators and computer screens.

This brave new bingo world has even spawned a new lingo. The holiday park company Butlins decided that the traditional number catchphrases used by callers were too *passé* for today's trendies so in 2003 they got Professor Charlie Blake, a 'popular culture' lecturer at University College, Northampton, to come up with some new ideas. Here's a primer:

Bang on the drum (number 71) becomes *J-Lo's bum*
Danny La Rue (52) becomes *chicken vindaloo*
Buckle my shoe (32) becomes *Jimmy Choo*
Reign of Queen B (73) becomes *camomile tea*
Dirty Gertie (30) becomes *Ali G*

And so on. Gimmicky it may be, but how many under-40s have ever heard of Danny La Rue? According to market research experts Mintel, almost half of all British bingo players are aged under 45 and 37 per cent of new members signing up with halls are 18–45. Among women the game is the single most popular leisure activity in the 20–25 age bracket.

And yet there's hope for purists who like their bingo in the raw. The *Daily Telegraph* reported how two grandmothers had been banned for life by the Castle Bingo Hall in Bridgend, South Wales. One had beaten the other to a 'lucky chair' and in the ensuing punch-up, watched by 500 bewildered players, the loser broke her rival's nose. 'I used to go to the club most nights and felt I knew everyone,' said one of the grandmas. 'Now I'm stuck in the house staring at the wallpaper. Even a murderer doesn't get life.'

Finally, if numbers are your thing, there are a couple of other punts worth exploring – premium bonds and the football pools. Like bingo, both have been written off as dinosaur products in the past. Suddenly, they have a new lease of life.

Premium bonds were introduced to Britain by Tory Chancellor Harold Macmillan (later Lord Stockton) in 1956. His not unreasonable idea was to bolster the economy through saving, although he faced an unlikely alliance of critics led by a young Labour MP called Harold Wilson and the Church of England. Wilson told the House of Commons that Britain's strength, freedom and solvency depended on 'the proceeds of a squalid raffle', while the Church claimed the draw was downright immoral. The hypocrisy of the Church's position was not lost on Macmillan, who gave a wonderfully understated recollection of events to the House of Lords during a debate on 4 November 1984. 'The Archbishop of Canterbury complained that I had "debauched the people",' he said. 'I suppose there must have been some confusion with the lotteries which they hold at church bazaars.'

During the 1980s and '90s, when UK interest rates hit 15 per cent, premium bonds seemed a poor bet. They couldn't possibly compete with the return on savings accounts. In 2003 things look very different. Invest £1,000 ($1,500) in a building society now and you'll be lucky to earn £25 ($37.50) a year in interest after tax. Stick the same amount into premium bonds and the odds suggest you'll win £50 ($75) over 30 months with the outside chance of bigger money or even the £1 million ($1.5 million) monthly jackpot. All this with no tax paperwork. Admittedly, the odds of a jackpot win are even worse than Lotto (it's 30,000-1 that you'll win a prize with any single bond), but of course you don't lose your stake money. Invest £5,000 ($7,500) and, with average luck, you've a 6-1 chance of winning twice a year courtesy of Ernie (Electronic Random Number Indicator Equipment), the National Savings & Investment bank's bond computer.

British punters seem convinced. Figures released by the UK Treasury on 9 May 2003 show that people are currently investing £19.9 billion ($29.85 billion) in premium bonds, or £330 ($495) for every man, woman and child in the country. This means the national stake has increased sevenfold inside ten years and 23 million Britons hold bonds. Not bad for a squalid raffle.

The football pools revival is still in its infancy, though confidence among operators is growing. For years the pools companies trogged along with the same old games in which punters had to predict 8 score draws out of 58 to be in with a chance of the jackpot. The idea that skill or soccer knowledge plays a significant part in this process is spurious to say the least.

One researcher logged the predictions of three professional newspaper pools experts. He discovered that where they unanimously tipped a score draw the actual success rate for those games was a meagre 5 per cent (*Gambling: A Guardian Guide*, Julian Turner, 1995). Shutting your eyes and using a pin will probably work just as well but before you hand in your coupon bear in mind that there are 2 billion, that's *billion*, sets of 8 matches you can select from 58.

The growth of the National Lottery during the 1990s all but destroyed the pools business. Total amount staked fell by 60 per cent between 1993 and 1999, and barely 8 per cent of UK adults are now regular players. Undeterred, the pools giant Littlewoods splashed out £1.35 million ($2 million) to snap up its main rival Zetters in August 2002. The deal added 60,000 punters to Littlewoods' client base of two million and gave it 85 per cent of the UK market. It may seem a strange gamble but then football, particularly the English Premier League, has become a global brand worth billions. In the world economy, companies see sport as a driving force.

And, in case you didn't know, there's now a worldwide way to bet on it...

02

WORLD

'Whoever concerns himself with big technology, either to push it forward or to stop it, is gambling in human lives.' - Freeman J Dyson, physicist

There are many unrealistic claims made for the World Wide Web but calling it a gambler's paradise isn't one of them. With a PC, modem and credit account you can bet every second of every day on everything from computerized greyhound racing to virtual dice; slot machines to stock markets.

You can call up the card for the last race at Sedgefield, compare odds between online bookmakers and stake a couple of grand with a click of your mouse. You can turn bookmaker and lay odds on a betting exchange. You can make live, running bets on soccer or American Football, selling in and out of your position as a game progresses. You can play poker and blackjack against computers or, if you must, against actual human beings. There's bingo, keno and the online national lotteries plus friendly online casinos that offer fun money to try roulette before you risk the real stuff. You can even spread bet on wars and the prospects for world leaders. All this at a time when interactive TV and the new 3G mobile phones are barely up and running. As that old Bachman Turner Overdrive song goes: 'B-b-b-baby you just ain't seen nuthin' yet.'

The one sure thing about online gambling is that it's a truly global industry. Given a power supply and a satellite dish you can run your casino or bookmaking website from the middle of the Amazon rainforest if you want. There are any number of offshore havens in which to shelter profits (bad news for governments that rely on gambling taxes) and barely a business overhead to worry about. There is of course the thorny issue of public health, particularly the risk to compulsive gamblers and young people, but if you're ten thousand miles from your markets do you really have to worry? Have politicians thought all this through and, if they have, will it make a dime's worth of difference? Well, maybe, just maybe.

In picking through the online maze, we need to look at the kind of gambling we're talking about. There are basically two types – betting on games of pure chance (such as the virtual slot machines and roulette games of online casinos) and betting on actual events (football matches, the stock market or the chances of Lord Lucan mounting Shergar to win the Epsom Derby).

This second category is the domain of the online bookmaker and involves, theoretically, some element of skill or knowledge. It can be sub-divided into fixed-odds, spread betting or – and this is *the* trendy way to bet these days – person-to-person exchanges. Of course all these betting propositions are accessible in traditional formats. Bookmakers won't be squeamish if you hand them cash over the counter, it's just that the Internet makes everything more convenient. It also makes it easier to cheat. There's more on global hi-tech crime – particularly sports betting scams – in the next chapter.

First, a few figures. A US review of research into the world's online casinos (Schauerte, M, 1999) showed that they took wagers worth $13 billion (£8.5 billion) and paid out $651 million (£434 million) to gamblers, three-quarters of whom were a hardcore group of some 300,000 Americans. There were 300 casinos worldwide netting an average revenue of $3–4 million (£2–2.6 million) apiece. Some 25 countries offered online gaming licences to operators.

Looking at these statistics you might think it's all another Internet damp squib. After all if, in the whole of 1999, 300,000 Americans accounted for 75 per cent of online bets it's hardly epoch-making. Then you discover that just a year later the estimated figure had risen to 4.5 million US cyber-gamblers, a quarter of whom were at it every day. By then, in the Caribbean alone, 1,500 web casinos had registered a domain name.

This is despite that awesome American monster known as the legal profession stamping its feet to stop Internet bets being placed with or by anyone – home or abroad. Online casinos risk breaking the Wire Act because in the Land of the Free you generally can't the telephone to bet across state lines. Seeing as gamblers are now doing exactly this to the tune of billions of dollars a year you do wonder whether America learned *anything* from Prohibition (see pp74–5).

The advertising of any form of gambling once fell into roughly the same category as promoting yourself as a contract child-killer, although in recent years judges have become slightly more liberal. In June 1999 the US Supreme Court overturned a ban on gaming commercials that had resulted in fines for Nevada TV stations. Internet casinos still need to tread carefully though. Any indication that they're trying to market their wares to a non-casino state will certainly bring the Sheriff round.

Europe is still some way off the e-casino pace although, led by Britain, it's making up ground fast. The research company Schema predicts that the UK will take half the forecast $15.4 million (£10.26 million) in total European online gambling turnover by 2005. Of the British slice, $6.4 million (£4.26 million) will come via the Internet and a further $1.7 million (£1.1 million) from interactive TV.

ONLINE CASINOS

Joining an online casino takes minutes. You register, supply your credit card details and download the software. Sometimes you'll need to make an initial deposit but many operators offer up to $100 (£66) as a 'starting bonus' to get you interested. After that you can play the second you log on. The graphics are fast, slick and accessible and there's no messing about with card shuffling or waiting for the roulette ball to complete its 12th lap of the wheel. All the games – typically slots, roulette, blackjack and poker – are governed by sophisticated software that generates the cherries, numbers and cards, and also fixes payouts.

Top prizes are big and getting bigger. One of the largest e-wins so far went to 'Jeffrey', a woman playing from home in Holland, who scooped $124,953 (around £83,000) in 2002 on an InterCasino virtual video slot machine called Aladdin's Lamp. InterCasino is one of the few online operators that has successfully set up both US and European websites.

According to the online *Gambling Times* (27 August 2002): 'Part of that success is owed to the painstaking detail the company applied to its Spanish and German sites. The language is not just translated, it's localised. It is detail like this that fuels European online gaming.'

The obvious fear is that the computers are rigged to take more of your money. But slots players don't fret about that in an arcade so what's the difference online? Of course, you might think twice about logging on to the Nigerian-based Easymoney-nevereverlose.com casino but you'd surely have no problem with familiar names like Ladbrokes, Victor Chandler, Aspinalls and Harrods. These companies have sound reputations, they can prove their software is audited and they can be held to account.

> 'The percentage of regular gamblers who become addicted is similar around the world. Estimates for the years 2000 and/or 2001/2 are as follows: New Zealand 0.5; Sweden 0.6; UK 0.7; Switzerland 0.8; US 1.1; Africa 1.1–1.4; Hong Kong 1.9.' Dr Howard Shaffer, *A Public Health Perspective On Gambling*

'It's all about making people feel comfortable,' says Russell Foreman, the launch boss of Aspinalls Online. 'There's no way we'd do anything to jeopardise our reputation' (*The Guardian*, 18 June 2001). In the same article Mark Brechin, author of a Mintel market research report on online gaming, agrees. 'People are very concerned by how easy it is to set up an online casino and then rip them off,' he says. 'That's why the brand is absolutely vital and why reputable brands have to operate transparent and audited casino websites.'

Herein lies the future of cyber-betting. Casinos will build a global image by registering in economically secure nations, with tight regulations. They'll get the gamblers' trust. And the nation states will get their taxes.

NO FEAR

At Salford University's Centre for Gambling Studies, Dr Greg Anderson says this is why the UK is keen to embrace online gaming. It is a position fundamentally at odds with Australia, which has already temporarily banned its citizens from gambling on websites based in their own country. Dr Anderson told me:

There is a lot of fear about online casinos but much of it is unrealistic. All we're really talking about here is new technology. Playing the game is pretty much the same. The big problem is to make sure that all the income doesn't go offshore.

That's the critical issue for governments. Revenue. If any business goes offshore there's a revenue loss. A lot of the stuff said about Internet gambling is as much to do with the taxation regime as anything else. Companies go offshore to avoid paying tax. If you bring them home, legitimize them and set them up properly to tap into bigger markets then they'll accept a tax burden on their profits. It's all about getting the tax balance right.

British ministers will eventually seek to fine-tune the regulations to make sure they accommodate UK operators. If you look at the Budd Report it's very clear that the aim is to bring online gaming into the same legal framework as mainstream gambling.

That's not to say the government could stop you setting up in the Bahamas or somewhere. But why would a customer go to you ahead of a UK site run by a company with proven integrity and probity? You'd have to offer such a tremendous price advantage it wouldn't make economic sense. Once you bring online gambling into the main national jurisdiction offshore operators will not have many advantages.

Anderson thinks most governments will be reluctant to interfere with e-gambling in people's homes – 'an enormous invasion of privacy' – and insists there can be no comparison with pornography. He points out that few of us have strong feelings about gambling whereas there is a clear popular demand for regulation of porn sites.

As for fears about problem gambling, particularly adolescents getting hold of a parent's credit card, he feels the risk is overblown. 'Internet banks have so far proved safe enough,' he says. 'Why can't online casino operators and bookmakers demand passwords, utility bills and checkable IDs to enforce security?'

Elizabeth George, head of the North American Training Institute and a leading opinion-former on gambling and health issues, agrees that the industry will get its act together. 'Certainly, little can be done so far to deter kids from gambling online,' she says, 'but there are some promising and sophisticated ideas.

'The Internet casinos are trying to develop technology which identifies users through thumbprint recognition or eye-scans. Companies know that without proper safeguards to deny children access, their industry has an Achilles Heel. At the moment this whole area is almost impossible to get your arms around. There is so much money involved and regulation is difficult.'

The online onslaught may carry major implications for traditional casinos but few experts believe they will crumble. At Casino Creations Vic Taucer thinks the real danger is that all gambling will eventually be shunned as anti-social, much in the same way that Americans now regard smoking in public places.

I don't see how casinos can avoid the competition. What do they say? That gambling is bad? Don't gamble online, come to us instead? They can't combat it so they'll have to work with it. Maybe they'll build a reward system into virtual outlets. You'll earn points for using the website and redeem these with a free flights and accommodation package at a casino.

To me, gambling is a social thing and the Internet destroys that ethos without offering anything in exchange. Gambling websites don't create many jobs, there's no social fun element, there's no revenue for government and yet there is a great new temptation and danger for addicts. Sooner or later these are issues we will have to address.

I'm not saying the Internet will be the downfall of the casino industry. Far from it. The downfall lies maybe 25 years or more away and it will be a backlash against the very idea of gambling. Historically there have always been swings of public opinion over whether it is socially acceptable. At the moment I think we've gone too far with the product without addressing the addictive problems. States will start outlawing it and look for other ways to raise revenue.

DOING IT YOURSELF

In the meantime though, why not launch your very own worldwide Internet casino? Not sure where to begin? No problem. Simply log on to www.startcasino.com for a series of helpful tips on what's involved. You could start by calling your house 'Pharoah Fortune'.

Startcasino opens with some reassuring advice on the danger of your clients winning big. For one thing, it says, casino software limits both individual and daily bets specifically to guard against this. Payout percentages are carefully tailored to safeguard your profits. Best of all it points out that '...what is commonly known as "the nature of gambling" indicates that most gamblers keep going until they are out of cash'. So that's all right, then.

You are then taken through the various options for budding e-casino owners. 1. Design and build your own software. Startcasino recommends you first save up several million US dollars for development costs. 2. Become a licensee of an Online Gambling Software Provider. This apparently costs anywhere between $30,000 and $1 million (£20,000-650,000) a year plus licensing fee (average $150,000 in the US). 3. Become a sublicensee. Much cheaper ($5,000-60,000 a year) but you do all the marketing and have to pay a big chunk of 'drop' (ie stake) royalties to your licensee.

Finally, under the headline 'When Would A Casino Become Profitable?', comes the rub. 'Keep in mind,' says Startcasino sagely, 'one needs to spend money to make money. A reasonable expectation would be to spend about $400,000-500,000 (c.£300,000) including the licensing fee and there should be a return on investment in approximately 9 months.'

It adds that most new online casinos have a monthly marketing budget of between $30,000 and $50,000 (£20,000-33,300) with established names allocating well over $1 million (£0.6 million). For the best performers annual profits are said to top $12 million (£8 million). But, the site warns: 'Do not think people just put down $250,000 and expect to make millions in return [sic].' This is sound advice. The fact that some e-casinos make money doesn't mean they all do. Like so many aspects of the dotcom business there are plenty of turkeys out there.

By the spring of 2002 the reality check for do-it-yourself gambling sites had kicked in. Analysts at the investment bank Merrill Lynch reported that for the first time in five years the number of worldwide online gambling sites fell slightly to 1,800. Most of the casualties seem to have been Caribbean or Central American operators.

'It's very easy to set up an online casino but it's increasingly difficult to make money out of it,' Ernst & Young's hospitality and leisure partner Iain Wilkie told the London *Observer* (7 April 2002). 'We're now seeing an industry fallout as the stronger players with the brands assert themselves. The smaller, opportunistic guys in places like Antigua or Costa Rica may have done well at first but most will be history.' Nigel Payne, chief executive of Sportingbet.com, put it like this in the same article: 'The Internet was global and as only 10 countries in the world have legalised betting shops suddenly every man and his dog thought "I'd like a bit of that".'

The correction in the market had a knock-on effect even on well-known names. Aspinalls Online admitted (April 2002) that a Bermuda-based e-casino it purchased the previous year for £30 million ($45 million) was almost worthless. And although Gaming Insight, the company that manages the Harrods.com casino, reported profits up 300 per cent to £12 million ($18 million) in the 18 months to the end of 2001, its share price plummeted over the following 12 months – from 25p to 6p. Investors enjoy gambling. But not at any price.

PLAYING PEOPLE

If you don't like pitting your wits against a computer online you can always take the old-fashioned route and play people. Poker websites offer glorified chat rooms in which you buy chips via credit card and play as though you were sitting round your kitchen table at home. The virtual cards are dealt by software, which is fine. But that software can't know whether your new best friends are phoning each other to exchange info on the hands they're holding. If they are, their simple little scam will be generously financed by you.

The bigger poker sites counter such collusion by monitoring betting patterns and checking players to see if they always join the same table. Watch out for anyone who hikes up the pot by re-raising (to get maximum bets out of you) even though he has a rubbish hand. Your cheat antennae should also waggle if someone folds despite a big pot with just one bet to go. At ukpoker.com Mark Strahan advises players to stick with established names such as Poker Stars, Planet Poker, Ultimate Bet, Paradise and Party Poker. There's also a site called Poker Pulse that logs the number of players using the top ten online cardrooms at any given moment. Strahan says:

It's supposedly a different game because you can't see your opponents and it's hard to judge if or when they're bluffing. Some players reckon that face to face you can second guess people by their eye movements, facial twitches, speed of breathing, the way they pick up their chips blah-de-blah-de-blah. Personally I think there's a bit of bravado in this. To be honest most of us have enough trouble looking at our cards and wondering what the hell to do with them.

If you're serious about Internet poker you probably should monitor your opponents' betting style. Money's money and no one likes to lose. Online if you know you've got the best hand you tend to bet everything. If you haven't got top cards you hold back.

ONLINE BOOKIES
Once upon a time a visit to your bookmaker essentially meant two things. 1. You wanted to back a horse. 2. Your bet would be at fixed odds, ie you knew precisely how much you'd pocket (or not) once the race was over. So if the geezer down the pub proved right in his advice to stick a tenner on Norfolk And Chance at 7-1 you knew you'd collect £80 ($120) from the bookie - £70 ($105) winnings plus your stake money.

Gradually things have got more sophisticated with the popularity of accumulator or combination bets - typically doubles, trebles and yankees - in which winnings from one race are automatically staked on a second and then third, and so on. This is considered a good way of winning big with comparatively small stakes, although punters conveniently ignore the vanishingly small chance of it actually happening. And once the bet is made it's written in stone. No good pleading with the bookie that as five of your six selections at Haydock have won you'd like to take the money and forget the 4.45! Oh no. You must just sweat in front of the TV and realise you've got 30K riding on the jumpy-looking nag with rolling eyes that is refusing to come under starter's orders.

Traditional fixed-odds bets are still popular but spread betting has added a new dimension. Bookmakers now offer odds for any sporting contest and thanks to their online services you can change your exposure in seconds as a match, racecard or tournament unfolds. Get it right and you can make huge sums of money unbelievably quickly. Get it wrong and the gutter looks an awful lot closer.

British spread betting evolved out of City wagers on gold prices. In 1974 the former metals trader and stockbroker Stuart Wheeler formed the IG Index to create a spread market in gold prices on a given day. Suppose IG set a 120–126 point fall. Gamblers who believed gold would plummet more than 126 could stake, say, £10 per point. If the index finished down 130 they'd make 4pts x £10 = £40. If it fell by only 110 then they'd lose £100 (10pts x £10).

The big advantage of the system was that it got round tough exchange rules on gold trading and was tax-free to boot. It also appealed to City traders' death-or-glory instincts. The better your reading of the market the more you won. The worse you performed the more you suffered. 'I'm a bookmaker and proud of it,' Mr Wheeler told the *Independent* (23 March 2002). 'It is very important you describe me as a bookmaker because we would not want to be confused with stockbrokers.' Heaven forbid.

Soon other companies moved in and spread-betting indexes emerged in shares, interest rates – even general election results. By the mid-1980s these businesses realized they could make a market in anything. As many City types had public school backgrounds (and were therefore cricket-friendly) cricket seemed a good place to start. Here was a sporting index ideal for whiling away those long, summer dog days when the Stock Market slumbered and lunches grew ever longer.

CRICKET, LOVELY CRICKET

Let's say you fancy a bet on the England cricket team's total runs in their first innings against Australia. Your bookmaker might quote 240–260. If you buy England runs you are backing the team to score more than 260. If you sell you reckon the Aussie's will steamroller them for less than 240.

Suppose you buy at £1 a run. Michael Vaughan goes in and spanks the Aussie pace bowlers around the ground to finish at 210 not out. Together the team amasses a first innings total of 420 and, hurrah and huzza, you're singing in the street at the prospect of collecting £160/$240 (420 minus 260).

However - and let's face it this is more likely - what if Glenn McGrath and his mates skittle England out for a humiliating 75? You've now finished 165 runs short of the spread and you owe your bookmaker £165 ($247.50). With hindsight, the right bet here was to 'sell' England runs.

Of course, the more you stake per run - or 'points' in spread betting parlance - the more you stand to win or lose. But at least you're not locked in. For one thing you can set a 'stop-loss', an instruction to the bookie that the bet is automatically closed when losses mount above a certain point. Or you can cash in your position via phone or Internet link at any time during the game (known as in-line betting) and take out a new one. This is where things get a touch more complicated.

As any sporting contest progresses so the spread will inevitably change. Take our Ashes example in which England were roaring away. It would have been nice if the bookie had continued to offer that 240-260 range right through their innings. But with England on, say, 261 for 3 wickets it wouldn't be great for business. Gamblers would be selling their grannies to take a bet that (a) couldn't lose and (b) might ensure early retirement. Were you to enter this betting market at

A 1996 survey by the Centre for Addiction Care in Breda, Holland, on the types of gambling treatment provided by 118 outlets in Europe, showed that individual therapy was most common (82 per cent). Second was family therapy (57 per cent) followed by group therapy (54 per cent) and debt restructuring (29 per cent).

261-3 and sought a quote on England's final runs tally you'd find the spread had moved way up - perhaps 390-410.

Betting in-line on this game then might have produced the following scenario. You know the Aussie bowlers are superb so you start by selling

England runs at £1 (also known as a down bet). You now have an open position on the 240-260 spread.

By the end of the first day you suspect you've got it wrong. The pitch is flat and true and England are 180-1 and cruising. Other in-line gamblers are now buying England runs and the bookie has responded by raising the '1st innings total' spread to 320-340. You decide there's no chance of a batting collapse and cut your losses by closing your position. This costs you £140/$210 (ie 320 minus 180 runs) but England seem on course for a big total which would push the spread above 400. You really don't want your exposure spiralling above £200 ($300).

Next day the weather changes. It's cloudy and humid and the ball could swing for the Aussie bowlers. Cricket gamblers clearly think so because there's an early rush to sell England runs. The bookie responds to market forces and the spread edges down before a ball has been bowled - to 300-320. You however are now convinced of Vaughan's form and you open a new position, now *buying* at £1 per run. Within the first hour of play the sun is burning down, the ball is gun-barrel true and England are again making hay. Their total of 420 means you have won £100/$150 on your second bet (420 minus 320) and cut your total losses to £40 ($60).

This is both the curse and blessing of in-line spread betting. The skill lies not so much in taking the bet but knowing when to close it.

There are countless other propositions to choose from. In cricket you might take a special on the England test spinner Ashley Giles; let's call it the 'Cash For Ash'. The bookmaker offers a points spread of 80-90 in which Giles earns 20 points per wicket, 10 points per catch and 1 point per run with a 15-point bonus for any sixes scored. If Giles claims four wickets, scores 20 runs and takes a catch anyone who buys Cash For Ash at £1 a point will be sitting on a £20 ($30) profit.

POINTS MEAN PRIZES

Spread betting is well suited to games settled by high numbers of points or runs, such as cricket, American football and basketball. American bookies work the spread slightly differently by drawing a 'line' - effectively a handicap - between two teams. Say they believe the Broncos are 15 points better than the Giants. They'll quote the Broncos at +15 meaning that if you buy you'll win at a fixed price of 11-10 on (ie you stake $11/£7.3 to win $10/£6.6) provided the Broncos secure that minimum 15-point winning margin. If there are more sellers than buyers the line will move down, perhaps to +12 or +10.

The bookmaker's aim is to achieve a balanced book with an exactly equal number of buyers and sellers. He makes his money by offering the 11-10 payout for what is actually an even-money bet. Punters meanwhile can open any number of new positions as the game progresses and their decisions will shift the line up or down accordingly.

As the sports spread-betting market has grown, so it has become more imaginative. Take soccer. With most games resulting in only two or three goals it's hard to run a normal spread. So the book is made up in tenths of a goal and you buy or sell the supremacy of one team over another.

Say Manchester United is at home to Chelsea. The bookies reckon the home side is a goal better so they quote '0.9-1.1 Man U over'. But you like the cut of Chelsea's jib and so you sell £20 ($30) of goals, a 'down' bet against Man U. Sure enough the visitors take a 0-1 lead inside 15 minutes giving you a profit of £38 (0.9 + 1 goal x £20). At this point the canny gambler can ensure he wins whichever team wins.

With Chelsea 0-1 up the spread has responded by dropping to minus 0.15 to plus 0.15. If you now buy Man U goals for £20 at 0.15 – an 'up' bet – you have effectively created your own spread (the difference between 0.15 and 0.9). If maths is not your strong point here's a couple of examples showing how you might fare.

Chelsea win 0-2. You win £58 on the down bet (0.9 + 2 goals x £20) and lose £43 on the up (0.15 + 2 goals x £20). Overall profit: £15.

Man U win 3-1, a supremacy of two. You lose £22 on the down bet (0.9 – 2 = 1.1 x £20). But you win £37 on the up (2 – 0.15 = 1.85 x £20). Overall profit: £15.

Other soccer bets are a bit easier to follow. You'll find spread markets in total goals, corners, throw-ins, the number of times a trainer comes on to treat injuries, the total of yellow or red cards, the tally of shirt numbers worn by scorers, and so on. If you know a team has two nippy wingers who love crossing from the dead-ball line then buying corners at 5–7 could be a canny move. Chances are, some hairy-arsed defender will come sliding in every time to boot out the ball and up your winnings. This is what turns genuine football fans into spread-betting tarts. If you're not careful you'll find yourself cheering your side's corners louder than you cheer their goals.

Gaming statistics for the state of Mississippi in April 1998 show that 37,937 slot machines accounted for 80 per cent of the $217 million (£145 million) profit shared between 29 casinos.

It's worth remembering that in a total goals market the spread eases down as the game wears on because there's less time for players to score. But betting will also reflect the fact that, in the English Premier League, more goals are scored in the second halves of games and the final minutes tend to be a particularly happy hunting time for strikers as defenders tire.

The latest version of in-line betting involves incidents – ie gambling opportunities – that occur during a game. It's already available in Britain through the Sky Sports channel's interactive service Sky Play, which allows viewers to predict whether a free kick will result in a goal, miss or save, whether an injured player is substituted, the chance of a tackle bringing a yellow or red card, which way the goalie dives on a penalty, and so on. If you're right you earn points and points mean cash prizes at the final whistle. There are even plans to use this principle during soap operas. Sportech, which has interactive betting rights across all the UK's ITV channels, wants viewers to bet on the eventual outcome of cliffhanger episodes.

In truth it's hard to see a mainstream sport, game or pastime that can't produce a spread market. Even the fixed-odds fortress of horseracing has succumbed through bets such as the 'favourites index' and here a bit of research can deliver excellent value. Essentially, the favourites in each race are awarded points for their finishing position – 25 for first, 10 for second and five for third. The index predicts the total number of points achieved by all favourites on the racecard for a specific day– let's say 49 points. If you sell the index at £10 ($15) per point you're banking on a bad day for the lot of 'em.

It's clear that sporting spreads and Internet betting were made for each other. The idea is now so mainstream that even the British royal family are on board with the Queen's granddaughter Zara Phillips sponsored by Cantor Index to pursue her equestrian career. If you have specialist knowledge, strong nerves and a healthy betting bank then playing online squeezes value out of your gambling. And the good news is that you don't always have to beat the bookmaker. Because you can be the bookmaker.

FAIR EXCHANGE
The betting exchange is the Internet's latest baby. It works in a similar way to Internet auction rooms where you post an item for sale, the buyer pays the webmaster, who pays you, minus a small commission. Equally, buyers can request an item and sellers will respond with a range of prices. The website guarantees the whole transaction and the market is worldwide.

Betting exchanges operate the same dynamics. Say you want to back Morning Tide in the big race. You've checked bookmakers' prices and you consider 9-4 to be miserly. So you log on to an exchange, request Morning Tide at 7-2 and wait to see if anyone will sell the bet. If they won't, chances are you've priced the horse wrongly. But, unless you're seeking really stupid odds, it's likely someone will take you up.

The reason is that there are thousands of racing fans playing the exchanges. Many may not share your view about Morning Tide and have earmarked four or five other good contenders in the race. So they turn bookmaker and post odds on your horse, effectively backing it to lose. They do this by lodging money with the exchange to cover payouts and then limiting the number of bets they'll take - eg £2,000 ($3,000) worth of stakes at 7-2. This means their total exposure to a Morning Tide win is £7,000 ($11,050).

Exchanges will give better odds because they don't have the same staff and business overheads faced by their traditional rivals. To cover costs and make a profit the high-street bookie has to price horses shorter than their actual chance dictates. In other words, a genuine 3-1 shot will be offered at 5-2. On the exchanges however the website operators make money charging a commission, usually between 2 and 5 per cent on all winnings. To gamblers, of course, this spells value. That's why they're logging on in droves.

Including Steve Lewis Hamilton. He reckons the exchanges not only treat punters better; they deter bookies from influencing the odds through big, on-course wagers. In the past this has been a neat way of manipulating the starting price, the course odds that off-track bookies are supposed to reflect. Let's assume you're a betting chain supervisor and your staff is taking big bucks on Flutter By. You want to cut the odds but, if you do, you might drive away business to other bookies who don't have the same financial exposure. Hamilton explains:

> In the old days, the bookie would send £3,000 to his runner at the track, back the horse and cut its odds from maybe 2-1 to 7-4. In that way he offsets his liability. If he tries the same thing now he'll find the on-course bookmakers back the same horse themselves on the betting exchanges. This covers their own liability and means they don't need to artificially cut odds.
>
> I've been involved full-time with racing for 13 years but the changes over the last three or four have been greater than anything over the last 100. All the old rules and philosophies are changing. The standard view was that the punter never won and you never saw a skint bookmaker. It's far from the truth now. Bookmakers used to win, not because they were good judges of horses but because they were good mathematicians. If you know your maths and your horses there's never been a better time to beat them.

Hamilton believes the big chains – Ladbrokes, Coral, William Hill – are deeply worried.

> The turnover on the exchanges is absolutely phenomenal. Bets are unlimited and it gives you an opportunity to lay off horses, which is actually illegal at the track. More important still is the competition factor. If you've got three runners in a race and they've each got an equal chance they should each be quoted 2-1. Typically, a bookmaker

will offer 7-4 to build in his profit margin. On the exchanges you'll get at least 2-1 and possibly better. This is because everyone out there has a different opinion and you can instantly make comparisons to get the best deal. It's the ultimate example of market forces working in the punter's favour.

If you're an expert on any sport there's no reason why you can't make it pay. You haven't got to worry about the bookmaker's cut – it's just your judgement against another punter.

Increased competition from the exchanges has led to innovative thinking from old established names, sometimes at a cost. Bet Direct, the betting arm of Littlewoods Leisure, has been in the vanguard of this touchy-feely attitude to punters, with special offers like one-quarter of the odds on each-way bets down to fifth place (instead of fourth). Usually these deals emerge for big-field TV handicaps such as the Cesarewitch, Cambridgeshire and, of course, the Grand National.

'One of our whizzy ideas was to pay back on the first fence fallers in last year's Grand National,' says Bet Direct's managing director Steve Taylor (in the *Racing Post*, 13 February 2003). 'At the time we thought there were six, which alone was a disaster, but in fact there were nine casualties including horses like Paris Pike and Marlborough. The average is less than two... The result of the race [a win for 20-1 Bindaree] was a good result for most bookmakers but we gave back more than half the money because of the concession.'

SELLING RISK

Despite better deals for punters, Hamilton isn't sure he likes the way professional gambling has changed with the turn of the century. He still finds himself rising at 5.30am to check form, only now he huddles over a PC rather than the formbook. Deep down, he reckons he needs to get out more.

In the old days I'd do the form work and still six days a week I'd be out at racetracks. Now I go once every couple of weeks because financially it makes more sense to work from home on the betting exchanges.

I'm not sure this is what I want to do with my life. One of the reasons I kicked off as a professional punter was that I loved racing and racecourses. If I'm stuck in front of a PC screen I obviously don't see the horses or get a feel for things. But I can't stop the march of progress.

The British-based exchange Betfair, which launched in 2000, shows just how quickly the march is going. It claims to be handling £2.6 billion ($3.9 billion) worth of bets a year, on which measure it falls behind only Ladbrokes and William Hill as the world's biggest bookie. Betfair says its 100,000 customers represent 90 per cent of the British exchange market and enjoy odds 20 per cent better than any high-street chain.

At the Dublin-based exchange TradeSports.com the emphasis is slightly different. Here they concentrate on global sports betting using a base currency of US dollars, a tactic that has wooed 20,000 regular punters over the company's first 18 months. Chief executive officer John Delaney says the aim is to service fans' desire to back or lay propositions at the best odds.

We know our USPs [unique selling points]. Better value by betting against other passionate players who don't need boookmakers' margins. Laying your own odds if you don't like what's on offer. But best of all is the excitement. Trading bets against others while a game is running is a fresh experience for many people. Even if you're only trading with £50, it's a whole new buzz. It's also appealing to successful punters who may find a bookie won't take their business.

I'm not a big gambler, in fact I come from the investment management industry where decisions are made for the long rather than short term. But on an exchange like TradeSports you will get good value on longer-term markets as well.

We look at it like this. A relatively small number of bookmakers sell bets and punters buy them. When you enter a betting shop or site you do not have bookies competing for your business. It's a take-it-or-leave it offer. On an exchange where you have a large number of buyers and sellers people intuitively know they'll get the best variety and the best value. That's one reason why e-bay is so successful. This is common sense stuff and punters know it.

A bookmaker, being a single seller, versus a large number of other sellers is always going to find it hard to compete. For one thing a private individual doesn't need a bookmaker's margin. The bookie has to charge for the bet he's selling you and that, by definition, will almost always be higher than on a liquid exchange as the bookie has to cover costs that a punter does not. The exchange is simply better and more efficient at facilitating people trading risk.

Delaney is convinced the British and Irish-based exchanges will be successful in America, not least because US punters will trust them more than existing offshore providers in areas like the Caribbean. But he points out that web gambling is not about winning market share *per se* in any one country; what counts is the gambling take from specific sports and games.

The impact of person-to-person betting in the UK is clear and well-documented. In the US it hasn't been as significant yet although there's no reason to believe things will be any different. Our exchange is dollar-based and our business is focused on the biggest sports on the globe – NFL [American football], basketball and soccer. We've targeted fan communities rather than a geographic area such as Ireland or the US or the UK.

In the US market a lot of the sports books are located in the Caribbean and those guys are big betters themselves. Are you more comfortable with a risk-neutral exchange like us or would you prefer to place your $10,000 at the start of a game with another big gambler who might have a vested interest in influencing the spread?

SADDAM FUTURES

Tradesports undoubtedly believes in its product but it hasn't been above the occasional publicity-seeking betting proposition. In September 2002 it opened a market on the prospects for Saddam Hussein's political future. If you believed he'd fall before the end of March you bought Saddam; if not, you sold him. Similarly, you could bet on his staying power through April, May and June.

The trading worked exactly like any other exchange, with punters opening and closing positions according to media news bulletins. But what if the war hadn't had a clear result? What if Iraq had been riven by internal fighting for months? Delaney says Tradesports would have handled this.

> We were offering a bet on whether Saddam was president or leader of Iraq on a certain date. If he's not viewed by the UN or recognized by other states as president or leader we can definitively state this and resolve the bet. We do our damnedest and utmost to make sure the language is phrased so that it allows for a definitive result. However there will be times when even the best lawyer in the world will be unable to legislate in advance for every eventuality.
>
> In that event we'd go to our contract rules and look at the language and intention of the wager, settle on all the reasonable facts and independent information. It's just like having a settlement committee on a financial exchange. There will always be the need for common sense and good judgement overlaid by lawyerly attention to detail. This applies whether it's a betting exchange contract or exchange members trading between themselves.

Lawyerly language. The very thought makes you shudder. Particularly in America where mass head-shaking and finger-wagging is holding back the online gambling business, costing Americans a fortune in lost taxes and making lawyers fabulously rich. Who'd have guessed that the nation that gave birth to the Internet would so quickly be trying so hard to suffocate it? As they say in British newspapers, you couldn't make it up.

AMERICA ONLINE AND THE TAX FACTOR

So what's the problem with America gambling online? Well, right-wing politicians don't like it on moral grounds. Left-wing politicians think it penalizes the poor. And both sides worry about health effects on young people. As usual, though, what we're really talking about here is tax revenue. Or rather loss of it. Just as the Australian government has become addicted to its slot machines, so American states are fiercely defending their casino habit.

In the previous chapter we briefly looked at the profits of US casinos. The American Gaming Association, which represents most of them, argues persuasively that casinos act as unpaid tax collectors, creaming money off every bet to boost state coffers. It's not a bad line to spin your loved ones as you head for the roulette tables. You're not gambling because you enjoy it; you're just fulfilling a sense of duty! And although, darn it, you keep losing on the red numbers at least some deprived kids will get a skateboard park!

Speaking generally, it's difficult to deny the importance of gambling to local US economies. As the 1999 National Gambling Impact Study Commission's (NGISC) final report says, 'As it has grown, it has become more than simply an entertainment pastime: the gambling industry has emerged as an economic mainstay in many communities and plays an increasingly prominent role in state and even regional economies.' Later on in the report, it is revealed that 'Research conducted on behalf of the commission confirms the testimony... of casino workers and government officials that casino gaming creates jobs and reduces the level of unemployment and government assistance in communities that have legalized it.'

NGISC also quotes from the Gambling Impact And Behaviour Study Report, published by the University of Chicago's National Opinion Research Center (NORC) in April 1999: 'Those communities closest to casinos experienced a 12% to 17% drop in welfare payments, unemployment rates and unemployment insurance.'

Despite this the Commission was clearly unhappy about some trends in America's gambling industry. It recommended better healthcare for the nation's estimated 5.3 million gambling addicts, a ban on legal betting in college sports events, a ban on online betting, tougher controls on lotteries, restrictions on Native American reservation casinos, a minimum betting age limit of 21 and a ban on political donations from the industry. Not exactly a green light for gambling is it?

Talking of political donations we should note that during the 1997–98 US Presidential election cycle, gambling businesses donated over $3 million (£2 million) to the Republican Party and just under $2 million (£1.3 million) to the Democrats. In fact gambling donations to the Democratic Party were greater than it received from most other business lobbyists – alcohol ($1 million), tobacco ($0.9 million), agribusiness ($1 million), oil and gas ($1.7 million) and chemicals ($0.5 million). Only the insurance industry coughed up more – around $3 million. The Republicans still got most of their money from the tobacco ($4 million), insurance ($8 million), oil and gas ($6 million) and chemicals ($1.7 million) sectors (figures: Common Cause, quoted in *The WAGER* newsletter, 20 April, 1999).

Publication of the NGISC report coincided with a Gallup poll showing that two-thirds of Americans believed gambling should be legal everywhere and that casinos offered clear economic benefits. Two-thirds thought sports betting led to games being fixed and just over half agreed that the US had a compulsive gambling problem. Mixed-message opinion polls like this add little to the debate, but they don't stop politicians from cherry-picking the facts that suit.

THE JAPANESE APPROACH

In Japan, where they know all about faltering economies, local governments in Osaka, Tokyo, Shizuoka, Wakayama and Miyazaki have been campaigning for the right to licence gambling venues. 'Casinos are powerful tourism resources,' they said in a joint statement (*Casino World*, 8 February 2003), 'and there are high expectations that the new gaming industry would have positive effects on the economy and create jobs'.

It didn't wash with the central Japanese government. Within a couple of weeks Yoshitada Konoike, the minister in charge of de-regulation zones, was quoted saying that 'many Japanese see going to casinos as gambling' (surely something lost in the translation there) and 'half of the Japanese think they should never be legalised' (which presumably means a big percentage think they should). As we all know, opinion poll questions matter more than the answers.

WINNERS AND LOSERS

Some academic studies have certainly been positive about gambling's economic impact. In Indiana de-regulation has seen gaming tax revenues rocket from around $10 million (£6.6 million) in 1996 to some $370 million (£246.6 million) four years later. In 1998 more people visited Indiana's casinos than Disney World. Gaming taxes brought in three times the state's revenue from cigarette tax. And the money spent on slot machines would have financed the budget for two years.

Given this exponential increase you'd expect to see some rise in problem gambling and debt levels. In fact a study three years later by the Indiana University Center for Urban Policy and the Environment could establish no such link. When researchers questioned 1,107 people filing for bankruptcy in the state barely 50 per cent reported gambling in the last year. That's a smaller percentage than was found in a random sample of Indiana adults. The survey showed that just 12 per cent of those questioned were classified as problem gamblers.

However the problem with so much gambling research is, inevitably, interpretation. Take the NORC report (see above) for the NGISC. This looked at social and economic indicators for 100 defined US communities. Data was gathered from 1980, when only five of them were within 50 miles of a gambling venue, to 1997 when the number had risen to 45.

In summary, the National Opinion Research Center concluded that having a casino in close proximity generally led to significant increases in casino spending per head (+237 per cent), construction revenue (+18 per cent) and hotel or lodgings revenue (+43 per cent). What's more, there were significant decreases in unemployment (-12 per cent) and the payout of social welfare benefits (-3 per cent to -17 per cent). There were no significant changes in levels of crime, bankruptcy, infant mortality or local government revenue. Restaurant income was the only clear casualty – down 19 per cent.

Reviewing the study in its *WAGER* newsletter (August 17, 1999), Harvard Medical School's Division on Addictions urged caution:

> How can social and economic impact be...measured? Can such costs and benefits be quantified in dollars? Are we gauging the impact on individuals, on the local economy or on the government? While one can state with precision the number of jobs created by the introduction of a casino to a local economy, how can we measure the change in an individual's quality of life? There may be no definitive answers to these questions.
>
> The data seems to suggest that the introduction of a casino is generally economically beneficial to nearby communities while having little impact on social indicators such as crime and public health. But as discussed above, NORC's efforts represent only one of many ways to measure the impact of gambling. It is entirely possible that a different methodology might yield wholly different results.

Too right. A paper titled 'Who Loses When Casinos Win?' (Grinols and Omorov, Spring 1996), published in the *Illinois Business Review*, looked at the type of spending that might be influenced by seven casinos in the state. The researchers also wanted to know how far away this influence could be felt and the extent to which it was comparable across different casino locations. They chose ten spending categories based on State of Illinois tax returns.

The results suggest it's too simplistic to claim that casinos boost local economies, period. They do and they don't. The study showed that consumer and business outlets within five miles of a casino logged an average gain across all categories of $170 (£113) per $1,000 (£600) of casino revenue. Yet when they cast their net between five and ten miles from the gambling action the same categories suffered an average $195

(£130) *drop* in income. The authors cautiously concluded that, generally, sales near casinos rose at the expense of those further away. They felt Illinois casinos were an unreliable aid to regional economic development.

Of course, this hasn't stopped the politicians taxing them, and in Illinois they like their casino taxes. Frank J Fahrenkopf Jr, chief executive officer for the American Gaming Association, says the state's policies have created a 'dire situation'.

'I am proud of how the taxes from our industry have helped benefit state and local communities across the country, providing the funds necessary for new school and library construction, transportation and infrastructure improvements and historic preservation,' he wrote in *Global Gaming Business* (April 2003). 'However, there is such a thing as killing the golden goose.'

> One need only look at the current state of the industry in Illinois for evidence of how an unreasonable tax increase on the gaming industry can inadvertently cause more harm than good. With its gaming industry already the highest-taxed in the nation, the Illinois legislature last summer approved a new gaming tax structure that required the industry to return a whopping 50 per cent of gross revenue over $200 million.
>
> Rather than benefiting the state with an influx of cash, the proposal sent shockwaves through the local industry and forced major corporations to withdraw or scale back planned investment projects in the state. In addition, the increases have served as a disincentive for casino operations in the state to expand.

He says a University of Illinois study on alternative proposals submitted by the casino industry shows there is another way. Under the plan *A Better Deal For Illinois* (the gambling business is never knowingly under-punned) restrictions on the number of 'gaming positions' at casinos would be lifted and the 50 per cent tax take scrapped. The university team said this would result in an annual increase of $365 million (£243 million) in state and local taxes, an injection of $2.2 billion (£1.46 million) into the Illinois economy and the creation of up to 50,000 new jobs.

In his article Fahrenkopf warns that 'unreasonable' tax inflicts a competitive disadvantage. 'Illinois casinos have lost a significant portion of their market share in the region,' he says. 'Lower taxes and fewer limits on the number of slots allowed on each property have allowed casinos in neighbouring states to spend more money on marketing, expansion and retention programmes than their Illinois counterparts.' Any schoolkid economist knows he's right. But it's not always the politicians that hammer profit margins.

MARKET FORCES

In 1998 the Las Vegas casino developer Sheldon Adelson gave an uncompromising speech to the International Gaming Business Expo. 'Today, here in Las Vegas,' he said, 'there is a syndrome in casino development that I call "Strip Of Dreams". That is the mentality that says, "If we build on the Strip then the customer will come no matter what we build." But the difference here is that we already have over hundred ballfields...no market is unlimited. Ours has room to grow but I personally don't believe it's unlimited.'

As the builder of Vegas's $1.4 billion (£930 million) Venetian casino resort you can see his point. More than 20,000 new hotel rooms were due to open in the city by 2001, bringing total room numbers to 125,000. This despite the fact that city hoteliers have struggled to make use of the 12,000 extra rooms that came on-stream between 1995 and 1998. As a result in 1997 Vegas bed occupancy dropped 4 per cent to 86 per cent. Las Vegas, and Nevada generally, is the home of the real rather than the virtual casino. But if the real casinos are already suffering from an overheated market what'll happen when their online pals *really* get going. This is why many politicians and gaming executives are so keen to enforce existing laws on Internet gambling. It's just that no one seems quite sure what the law says.

According to one of America's leading authorities on gaming legislation, Professor I Nelson Rose of California's Whittier Law School, fewer than 25 people had been prosecuted for online gambling by the end of 2001. Of these, most were bookies taking sports bets across state lines. Professor Rose points out that gambling businesses which conduct all their trade inside a single state do not violate the dreaded Wire Act, whether they work on- or off-line. Passed back in the 1970s, the Act is designed to enforce anti-bookmaking laws by preventing legal bookmakers in one state taking telephone bets from clients in another that bans gambling.

Despite this there's no federal offence in placing an online bet provided the state where you live and the state where your bookmaker trades both accept interstate betting. Under Senator Jon Kyl's first draft Internet Gambling Prohibition Act such gambling would have been illegal but the US Justice Department made very clear that it wouldn't be chasing every $5 online bettor in the country, thanks all the same!

> **More than 80 per cent of Turkish compulsive gamblers bet to escape personal problems. This compares with 33 per cent of non-addicted gamblers. The survey of 73 men (Duvarci & Varan, 2000) also reported that 74 per cent of the compulsive players felt guilty about their addiction.**

'The major weakness of the Wire Act, beside the fact that it was written long before the Internet was invented,' says Professor Rose, 'is that it was designed to go after illegal bookies. Betting on a sports event or horse race is clearly covered. But a good argument can be made that lotteries and casinos do not fall under the Wire Act, even if they are conducted interstate or internationally (www.GamblingAndTheLaw.com, 12 November 2001).

As you might expect, different states are taking different views. The situation is further complicated because betting on professional and college sport is legal only in Nevada (see 'Money', p171) – and then only if the bettor is present or calling within the state.

On 11 June 2002 the New Jersey Attorney General David Samson announced he'd settled civil court cases against two e-betting operations after they agreed measures to stop New Jersey citizens placing sports bets. 'These settlements are an important step in protecting the citizens of New Jersey from the dangers of gambling on unregulated Internet websites that are not held to the stringent regulatory standards of our Atlantic City casinos,' said Samson. Cynics might feel this is a roundabout way of saying, 'stop thieving our tax money'. Samson's press release did however acknowledge that the New Jersey Assembly was in the process of setting up an Internet gambling commission to consider the impact of legalization.

CALIFORNIA SCHEMIN'

California has gone to the other extreme. In 2002 Governor Gray Davis approved possibly the second-largest expansion of legal gambling in America's history, allowing 34 million citizens to bet on authorized horse races out of state, either by phone or PC. The new law also allows licensed OTB (off-track betting) operators to accept bets from anyone in any state. Given the size of California's gambling market it's already clear that other states will have to produce similar legislation, or watch tax revenue tumble. And once American bookmakers and casinos get a proper foothold in the domestic online market it will be the kiss of death for small, offshore operations.

At the moment, though, most state legislatures – whatever the pros and cons of tax takes, economic boosts and the law – prefer the devil they know. For their part, casinos like the cozy certainty of the status quo. If you're a regular casino visitor in New Jersey you might nip down to Nevada once a year for a holiday but you're hardly going to bother with special offers and deals on a week-to-week basis.

On the Internet, things are very different. E-casinos compete instantly and aggressively with the added convenience of gambling from home. Even if you love the atmosphere of the craps pits or roulette table there's a good chance you'll place some of your business online. Operators will start asking why they should pay 50 per cent tax in Illinois when they can shop around the Union for a more welcoming rate or log on to that much-respected old ally, Great Britain plc. Gaming giant MGM has already run this idea up the flagpole by buying an online casino licence on the Isle of Man, a tax haven off England's west coast.

Of course, a US state will still be able to exert some control over adverts – a powerful weapon given that online casinos live or die by marketing. But going after advertising is fraught with legal pitfalls, not least the US Constitution's First Amendment right to free speech. Besides, adverts can be beamed direct to mobile phones or via foreign satellite TV or radio.

Passing a law against all this is one thing; enforcing it quite another. If you were a US state governor or casino boss wouldn't *you* be worried?

Hi ho, why is life so complicated? Oh for the days when you could gamble without a taxman or lawyer in sight. It did happen, but you need to go a *long* way back...

03

HISTORY

'If you can make one heap of all your winnings/ And risk it on one turn of pitch and toss/ And lose, and start again at your beginnings/ And never breathe a word about your loss' - Rudyard Kipling, 'If'

Gambling is driven by technology and economics. The online revolution, interactive TV, the intricacies of sports and spread betting, the mind-numbing minutiae of form guides and odds tables – all of it nurtures an image of sophistication and high science. To hear some pundits you'd think gambling began, like sex (according to Philip Larkin), 'in 1963...between the end of the Chatterley ban and The Beatles' first LP'.

In fact betting has a long and fascinating history. It isn't impossible to imagine your typical Neolithic hunter-punter, temporarily secure in food and shelter, chilling out with a little entertainment. Propositions may have been limited to flies climbing a wall but upping the ante by four arrowheads and a cowrie shell must still have made for a tense moment. It's not really so fanciful bearing in mind that gaming sticks have been dated as early as 6000 BC.

What is clear is that opportunities to gamble were abundant and that gambling itself was viewed very differently. Ancient punters had no idea about the mathematics of chance (given the appalling odds accepted by today's lottery players, evolution hasn't changed things) because they didn't accept that chance existed. According to many primitive cultures, apparently random events were actually messages from deities.

Ancient mythology often portrays 'hero gamblers' protecting their people against evil spirits, and this interaction between humans and the supernatural was also key to the divination business. It was well exploited by the priestly classes who jealously guarded their monopoly on cozy chats with the gods.

This isn't to say that divination was considered an absolute truth – or even taken seriously. There's plenty of evidence to show that ancient priests questioned deities not to *see* the future but to establish whether a desired result would actually *happen*. If they got the wrong answer they tried again until the gods came up trumps, so to speak.

It was the French anthropologist and philosopher Lucien Lévy-Bruhl who argued that primitive people believed a thing could be simultaneously itself and something else. While this may sound like the enlightenment of a lengthy LSD experience, the logic can be applied to early divination. On one level it was a chinwag with destiny; on another a betting opportunity. The point is that gambling games didn't necessarily evolve out of religious ritual. More likely, the two were intertwined right from the off.

An interesting example of this is the Ball Game, thought to have been invented by Olmec priests in the second millennium BC. A cross between Spanish pelota, basketball and volleyball, it was fought out on an H-shaped pitch in which two high walls were separated by a centre line. The aim was to bounce a rubber ball into the opponent's half, using knees, hips and elbows to keep it aloft. A person could win instantly by nudging it through one of two 20ft (6m) -high stone hoops – tricky considering they were only slightly larger than the circumference of the ball itself – but the bonus for a successful hooper was impressive. He was allowed to take all the possessions (including the clothes) of anyone he could catch in the crowd. Those were the days when spectator participation really *meant* something.

'God is all, while chance and circumstances, under God, set the whole course of life for us.' Plato

The game was later adapted by the Olmec's successors in central America, the Mayans, who further concentrated the minds of players by ritually executing the losing team. Much later (c 14th century AD) the Aztecs produced their own religious version in which the pattern of play was thought to predict the future – a clear example of the symbiotic relationship between the sacred and profane.

In many cultures deities themselves take the hand of fate. The Greek gods Zeus, Hades and Poseidon divided up their realms by drawing lots while Hermes, messenger of the gods, won five days from the moon goddess Selene (so fixing the calendar at a 365-day year). Greek historians noted that Zeus and Aphrodite could be contacted by tossing dice and, according to the great Indian Sanskrit poem the *Mahabharata*, the world is a dice game between a Hindu deity and his queen. This epic includes a character called Yudhisthiva who gets a bit carried away. During one game he bets 100,000 gold coins, 1,000 elephants, his entire staff of slaves, his army, his brothers and his wife.

PLAYING FUTURES

Divination could be a messy business. Inca priests pored over marks on a sacrificed llama's lung, while Babylonians preferred poking around in animal livers. The Etruscans of northern Italy relied on the flight of birds, the Chinese analyzed cracks in turtle shells and the Hindus saw future events in cloud formations. But globally there was one method that transcended all others – casting lots.

Originally this involved tossing sticks, animal bones or arrows into the air as a priest put questions to the gods. The way the objects fell determined the answers. This system was linked to the drawing of lots to determine awards or prizes, a scenario described in the Bible as the method used to divide Canaan among the Israelites. 'And the Lord spoke unto Moses saying...the land shall be divided by lot... According to the lot shall the possession thereof be divided by many and few' (Numbers 26:55).

There are other examples, among them the election of a king by lot (1 Samuel 10), the division of family lands (Isaiah 34:17) the assignment of priestly duties to Zechariah (Luke 1) and, most notably, the allocation of Christ's garments among the soldiers who crucified him (John 19: 23–4). Curiously, lots were used in Arabian public trials to decide guilt or innocence long after Islam specifically outlawed gambling and games of chance. This is perhaps a legacy of Ancient Greece; the Greek word for justice is dike, derived from the verb 'to cast'.

Early Judaeo-Christians had no problem with lots because they weren't seen as gambling paraphernalia but rather a revelation of God's will. It was only later that European bishops began to view gaming as a shortcut to damnation. Huge swings in public attitude are a curious feature of gambling down the ages, as we'll see.

Many traditional playing implements – dice, cards, dominoes, even chessmen – can be traced back to lot casting. The earliest wagers involved guessing challenges (in which partially hidden sticks or arrows were marked to denote rank) or games of chance (in which the throw of shaped sticks, bones or dice produced a winner). The fact that the laws of probability had not been invented mattered little to gamblers although even the dimmest must have noticed how much easier it was to throw a seven with two dice as opposed to a two or twelve.

Forms of dice were one of the first, if not *the* first, gaming tools used by humans. Excavations at burial sites in the Americas, Africa and eastern Asia have recovered simple oblong gaming sticks dating from 6000 BC and dice remained the gambling implement of choice right through to medieval times. Seeds, peach stones, animal bones, walnut shells and pebbles were all used in various forms but the birthplace of the modern die is thought to be the Orient. Here Korean Buddhists designed a type that bore magic spells and instructions for a game that reflected hopes of a better rebirth. Early Indian dice were used for studying *ramala* (seeing the future).

Sophocles, one of the great tragic dramatists of Ancient Athens, claimed dice were invented at the Siege of Troy by Palamedes. We can safely rule this out on the basis that Palamedes is a made-up character in Greek mythology. The historian Herodotus reckoned they were fashioned by the Lydians as a way of keeping minds off a terrible famine, while the Greek writer Plutarch gave the credit to the Egyptians.

GAME PLANS

There is certainly artwork in 4,000-year-old Egyptian tombs and temples showing board games being played. The earliest known board, discovered at a burial site near El-Mahasna, Upper Egypt, dates to the fourth millennium BC. It was accompanied by 11 cone-shaped pieces and is similar to versions in later tombs marked with ten rows of three cells. The game is known as Senat and, despite various attempts to work out the rules, no one's quite sure what you're supposed to do. Bit like spread betting, really.

Other early, and equally unclear, games include Hounds and Jackals (an Egyptian race game similar to snakes and ladders), the Royal Game of Ur (a kind of backgammon), the Gezer game (a plaque containing lots of holes found at Gezer, Palestine), the elaborate 4,000-year-old Knossos board game played by Crete's Minoan civilization (just looking at the board does your head in) and the Welsh *gwyddbwyll*, also known as *fidchell* in Ireland (no physical evidence it existed but it rates a passing mention in ancient texts).

Moving east we find the ancient Indian game of *ashtapada*, or 'eight-square', an early forerunner of chess and its slightly larger equivalent *dasapada*. The growth of the silk route encouraged an exchange of ideas as well as commercial goods and India exported several race-style games to China, among them the wonderfully named *t'shu-p'u*.

The Chinese philosophers Confucius (551–479 BC) and Mencius (371–288 BC) write of a game called Yih, better known in Britain as Three Men's Morris. The aim is to place and subsequently move three counters to form a row along eight marked lines laid out in a star shape. A major flaw is that as long as you go first, have a spark of nous and put a counter on the middle point you can't lose. If you're ever challenged to a game insist on playing the 'French Rule', which prohibits this tactic.

Roman soldiers were fond of *latrunculi*, played on a checked surface with an apparently unlimited number of pieces. Archaeologists have found remnants of these boards in mile castles along Hadrian's Wall and, in a synchronistic twist of history, they bear an uncanny resemblance to the modern Japanese game of *hasami shogi*.

DICING MANIA

It's possible, though unlikely, that the above games were played for the crack rather than hard cash. However, there's clear evidence that gambling games were prevalent by the time of Christ, that the Romans were driving the market and that shooting dice was closest to their hearts. The best throws they named after the goddess of love (Venus) and the worst were referred to as a 'dog', perhaps giving rise to that old nugget of folklore 'every dog has its die'. Or not.

One of the most prevalent Roman dice games was called *duodecim scripta* (12 lines), another ancestor of backgammon. Excavations at Pompeii, the town buried beneath volcanic ash during the AD 79 eruption of Vesuvius, revealed two paintings of this game in progress. Displayed in a tavern, the first shows two men sitting between the board. One is holding a dice cup and saying, *'Exsi!* [I am out!]'. The other retorts, '*Non tria, dvas est* [Not three, it's two!]'.

The second painting shows the two players standing to exchange punches as the innkeeper shows them the door with the words: '*Itis foras rixsatis* [Go outside if you want to fight].' The lesson for today's gambler is that even if you went to a decent independent school and got past *amo amas amat* in Latin, it won't help if you antagonize the local publican by dobbing your cribbage opponent in the bar.

Cubic dice known as *tesserae*, usually with today's arrangements of dots, and *tali*, an oblong version with four numbered sides, were Greek imports to the Roman world. They were the perfect tools for reckless gambling (a mark of both character and status) allowing rash, instinctive bets with the assurance of an instant result. Betting was woven into the fabric of life as is evident from the number of game layouts crudely etched onto plinths, public porticos and basilicas. If you or I see a flat surface we think 'table'. To a Roman, it said 'let's bet'.

As the Empire descended into decadence, gambling became a mania that could make or break its citizens. Lotteries were common and sports betting (particularly on chariot racing) became so widespread that at one point it was confined to the December Saturnalia festival. The barking mad Emperor Nero was said to have wagered 400,000 sesterces a point (roughly £10,000 in today's money) during a game of *duodecim scripta*. If you lost to Nero it was a good idea to pay up quickly. He had an unsettling habit of illuminating his palace gardens with burning Christians.

HEAVENLY TORTURE

For the gambling poor there was sometimes nothing left to lose but their liberty. In his *Germania* the historian Tacitus talks of conquered barbarians dicing for freedom:

> They play at dice...making a serious business of it; and they are so reckless in their anxiety to win...that when everything else is gone they will stake their liberty on a last decisive throw. A loser willingly discharges his debt by becoming a slave.

Suetonius tells how Augustus handed out stake money to dinner guests for the Chinese game of odd-even, Commodius turned the imperial gaff into a casino, Claudius diced while travelling in his carriage (and even wrote a book titled *How To Win At Dice*), Julius Caesar rolled 'em to test the fates before crossing the Rubicon and of course Mark Antony tossed regularly with Cleopatra at Alexandria.

Occasionally this imperial obsession was ruthlessly satired. In his *Apocolocyntosis Divi Claudi* (*The Pumpkinification Of The Divine Claudius*) the Roman dramatist and philosopher Lucius Annaeus Seneca describes the deified emperor being tortured by the gods. Claudius's eternal punishment for a lifetime of gambling was to throw dice from a bottomless cup.

> When from the rattling cup he seeks to throw
> The die they trickle through the hole below
> And when he tries the recovered bones to roll –
> A gambler fooled by the eternal goal –
> Again they fool him; through his finger tips
> Each time each cunning die as cruelly slips

By the first century AD, *duodecim scripta* had been modified into a slightly shorter version called *tabula* (also known as *alea*). This proved massively popular throughout the Roman Empire, to the point that the Church intervened to castigate the masses for indulging in something that looked suspiciously like fun. Canon 9 of the Synod of Elvira, Spain (c AD 305), attacked the playing of tabula for money and a decree added to the Justinian Code in the eighth century AD prohibited the clergy from indulging. The Russian Church later prohibited everyone, stating that 'no clergy or layman shall play at *zerniyu* [hazard], *shakhmate* [chess] or *tablei* [tabula]'.

Part of the Church's logic seems to have been that gambling detracted from good, healthy outdoor pursuits such as field sports and, especially, archery. Given the unstable political map a fit male population was vital. How could you quickly train a soldier to handle a longbow if his usual exercise centred on drinking and dice?

There was also an inbred belief that gambling caused public disorder. The great unwashed peasantry couldn't handle themselves like proper gentlemen when playing games of chance and so they had to be stopped. One striking example came in an edict to King Richard I's army as it headed for the Crusades. If you ranked below a knight, you were banned from playing dice, period. Knights and the clergy could have a bet as long as they didn't lose more than 20 shillings a day (offenders had to pay 100 shillings to the army's archbishops).

Monarchs could gamble whenever they wished (and lose as much as they wished) but their courtiers were restricted to the 20 shillings rule. Courtiers who lost more than this could be 'whipped naked throughout the army for three days', which seems a bit harsh considering the knights and priests got away with paying a fiver. But, that's the English upper classes for you.

Suppression of gambling during the Crusades provides an excellent example of why bans rarely work. The great irony is that playing cards – more of which later – only took off in Europe after King Richard's Christian soldiers were introduced to their Islamic foes. The Arab troops played to pass the endless hours of impossibly long sieges and, inevitably, those taken prisoner began dealing their captors in for a hand or two.

CHANCE ENCOUNTERS

From the 16th century mathematicians intrigued by the mechanics of gambling began having a Big Think about chance and probability. Officially these concepts still didn't exist – the Spanish Inquisition took a dim view of the idea that God wasn't directing everything – but the rise of international commerce provided a conduit for more open thinking. Merchants wanted insurance for their ships and insurers wanted to know the chances of a claim.

The Italian mathematician Pacioli used his knowledge of Arabic algebra and arithmetic to prepare the groundwork for the Probability Theory but it was his compatriot Gerolamo Cardano (1501–76) who made the early running. Cardano was a doctor, astrologer and mathematician but above all a fanatical gambler fascinated by the fall of the dice. In his *Liber de ludo aleae*, he concluded, 'I am as able to throw 1, 3 or 5 as 2, 4 or 6. The wagers are therefore laid in accordance with this equality if the die is honest.'

This was fine as far as it went, ie not very far, but the snag with Cardano's maths was that every face on the dice should have turned up once every six throws. As this patently didn't happen he was forced to add a caveat suggesting that luck played a part, something most tavern dice players had worked out for themselves. There are few prizes for half-right theorems but at least Cardano alerted the world to the problem. Sadly his later life was bedevilled by family tragedy and, according to one apocryphal tale, he was so horrified at failing to predict the date of his own death that he committed suicide.

It wasn't until the mid-17th century that the brilliant French mathematician and philosopher Blaise Pascal (1623–62) got to the nub of probability. Pascal was a follower of Jansenism, a sect within the Roman Catholic Church which held that the fate of all individuals was pre-destined by God. When he was challenged by a gambling friend, the Chevalier de Mere, to mathematically re-distribute stake money in a game that had been interrupted, Pascal came up with his treatise 'A Problem About Games Of Chance Proposed To An Austere Jansenist By A Man Of The World'.

Years earlier, both Pacioli and Cardano had had a go at something similar. They assumed that the pattern of the game up to interruption was a fair indication of what would have happened afterwards. In other words, players losing would continue to lose; winners would carry on winning.

Now, those of us who have cheered home a long-odds winner in the first race at Kempton, and reinvested it on a succession of donkeys thereafter, know this to be false. Pascal knew it too and he decided that the game was like an unfolding story in which nobody could foresee a late twist in the plot. His clear message, which generations of gamblers have since wrestled with, was that in truly random events the past has no bearing on the future. If you roll three sixes in succession the chances of rolling a six again remain exactly the same – one in six. For Pascal the solution to his friend's poser was that the division of stake money should ensure that each player believed it was in his interests to carry on with the game.

If this seems a cop-out bear in mind that today's computer-assisted mathematicians have come up with an equally frustrating formula to decide the result of interrupted cricket matches. Known as the Duckworth-Lewis method its principal advantage is that nobody understands it, ensuring that cricketers don't argue when it tells them they've lost.

ROLLING ODDS

In 1654 de Mere came up with another tricksy teaser for Pascal. He'd made serious profits by betting his gambling-mad cronies even money that he could throw a six in four attempts. They eventually got bored of losing so he agreed a slightly more complex bet; even money that he could throw a double six in 24 attempts with two dice.

The probability seemed the same. There are six possible outcomes of a single dice roll compared with 36 possible outcomes when two are used. The probability of getting a double six with two dice should therefore be 1 in 36 according to de Mere's reasoning. Unfortunately his losses suggested otherwise.

The problem was the same that had baffled Cardano a century earlier. De Mere's logic would have been fine if he was guaranteed to roll a double six once every 36 attempts. But of course a one in 36 chance doesn't promise that. It might take 72 attempts or 100 or you might be rolling forever and still not manage it (unlikely but theoretically possible).

Pascal worked out that the true odds, as in most probability issues, should be based on the chances of something *not* happening. In other words, what was the chance of de Mere *not* rolling a double six in a single throw? The answer of course is 35/36. So in 24 attempts the true odds are 35/36 x 35/36 x 35/36 etc 24 times – a result of 0.508596.

Put another way, 50.9 per cent of the time de Mere would fail to roll a double six in 24 attempts while 49.1 per cent of the time he would succeed. This meant he would lose 1.8 per cent of the total wagers (50.9 minus 49.1). Got all that? Here endeth the probability lesson. If you're still awake, you might like to know that de Mere actually needed 24.6 rolls to have an evens chance of winning. His experience should be burned into the brain of every gambler. Respect the odds, and they will respect you.

GAMBLING ON GOD

Before leaving Pascal it's worth noting how he used his theories on wagers, probability and gambling to show that a belief in God is reasonable. I only mention this because it's worth throwing into the mix during drunken, late-night arguments in the pub.

'Pascal's Wager' works like this: God either exists or he does not. If he does, belief in him offers the chance of paradise whereas disbelief leads to damnation. If he does not exist then believing or disbelieving makes no difference anyway.

Since paradise is the best possible result, and damnation the worst, it is reasonable to believe. Wagering that God exists – even if the chances are vanishingly small – produces such a huge payoff if true that it's mathematically worth the punt. In contrast, betting against God produces no reward whatsoever if you turn out to be right. You won't even be around to say. 'I told you so.' Worse, if you're wrong, there may be an eternity in hell in which to reassess your gambling strategy. Why Church leaders haven't tried this Pascal thing before is beyond me. It's what racing pundits call a 'value' bet.

Throughout the 17th century Europe's leading mathematicians shaped and honed Pascal's ideas. The Dutchman Christiaan Huygens, Switzerland's Jakob Bernoulli and France's Abraham de Moivre were among those who used gambling as a key to unlock probability theory. Concepts such as the law of large numbers, standard deviation and the law of averages began to emerge.

Essentially, scientists found they could predict the long-term but not the *immediate* result of a given act. No one could say which way a single, flipped coin would land. But if you flipped the coin 100,000 times the laws of probability and average would kick in to ensure the heads/tails split was close to 50–50.

Standard deviation is an important factor because flipping a coin 100 times is fairly unlikely to produce exactly 50 heads. Deviation allows there to be a *predictable* variation on either side. In fact, if you were so dull as to spend a day flicking a coin 100 times every hour, on the hour, you'd find that around two-thirds of the time you'd get between 45 and 55 heads.

There is a whole, mind-boggling debate here about what is strictly *pure* chance but, well, let's not go there. As gamblers, all we really need to know is that probability describes the likelihood of a chance event happening, as expressed in fractions, percentages or odds. Chance events do not include horseracing because this is influenced by the horse, its rivals, the track, the going, the jockey and whether or not the trainer's taken a bung. We haven't the space here to properly analyze the vagaries of racing odds so if punting on horses is your thing you'd be well advised to research a detailed strategy.

The effect of mathematical laws on the serious gambling student can hardly be overstated. By understanding the principles of probability a canny player can acquire an edge on the House or rival players simply by knowing the odds advantage of any given position. Take blackjack, a card game in which the aim is to draw cards as close as possible to the value of 21 – beating the dealer in the process. Any hand going above 21 is bust.

The odds flesh out like this. If the dealer reveals a 6 before betting starts, the odds of him going on to 'bust' are an attractive 42 per cent. But if he shows a 7 the probability drops dramatically to 26 per cent. This may not sound epoch-making but, in gambling terms, improving your chances by 16 per cent is the equivalent of free money. It doesn't mean you'll win every time but if you play long enough, and your strategy is right, you can acquire the edge.

But we're getting side-tracked. There are plenty of other books that promise to make your fortune at cards and thankfully my record at brag, poker and blackjack has ensured this isn't one of them. Time for some more history.

NEW DEALS

Like dice, cards owe their existence to fortune telling. At some point over the last six millennia prophets began using flat sticks decorated with symbols and once paper was invented by the Chinese in the second century AD it was only a matter of time. According to the German author Detlof Hoffman in his book *The Playing Card* (Leipzig, 1972) 'the game of cards appeared in the middle of the Tang Period, ie in the seventh or eighth centuries [AD].'

The birth of modern cards developed a little later, possibly via oiled paper strips produced in Korea during the 12th century AD. These were known as *Htou-Tjen*, or fighting arrows, and were used to predict the future. Later they bore an adapted Chinese design in which four sets – coins, strings of coins, myriads of coins and tens of myriads – comprised a pack. At the time these were familiar picture symbols used on paper money.

The importance of the number four in early religion seems to have been a worldwide phenomena. Perhaps it reflected a perceived natural order of things such as the seasons, points of a compass and the Four Noble Truths of Buddhism. Korean Hapkido martial artists even talk of an opponent's body having four 'corners' (essentially the shoulders and knees), which are considered key points of weakness.

Some early Indian cards used four suits depicting the Hindu god Ardhanari clutching a cup, sceptre, sword and ring. More popular though was a ten-suit pack known as the *dasavatara*, which was based on the ten incarnations of another Hindu deity, Vishnu. These were a fish, tortoise, wild boar, lion, dwarf, axe, bow and arrow, thunderbolt, conch and horse. If only it had taken off in Europe. Bridge would seem so much less stuffy if the bidding opened with three thunderbolts.

Initially, card playing tended to be a preserve of the rich. Each card had to be hand-painted or carved, and often a nobleman would commission likenesses of his own family, property or lands to appear in the pack. Wood-block printing and stencils helped cater for a wider market but it wasn't until the printer Johannes Gutenberg pioneered movable type in Germany during the 15th century that cards took off as mass-produced gambling phenomenon. The advantages were obvious. They were portable, simple to understand and offered a huge range of games.

The claim that Arabs introduced playing cards to Europe has some etymological support. Ancient documents refer to them as *naibi* and one early Arab pack contains a card called a *naib*, a derivative of the Arabic word for prophet. In Italy, where fortune-telling tarot cards first appeared in the 14th century – perhaps imported by Marco Polo – cards are still known as *naibi*. In the tarot we again see how games and mysticism can sit comfortably together.

Tarot symbols were regarded as heathen by the Roman Catholic Church so, in a sop to the bishops, the Venetians 'Christianized' them with suits based on the Italian social classes. Following the four-suit Chinese tradition, Venetian cards carried curved swords (the nobility), cups (the Church), money (merchants) and clubs (peasants). Each was ranked in military hierarchy with kings as the top picture card followed by knights, valets and the arrow-fodder of faceless troops from ten to ace.

Later Europe's ruling families introduced further adaptations using heraldic symbols of power and wealth. It is thought the French established the modern 52-card pack by axing the 22 'triumph' cards from tarot decks and removing the knights. The four suits became *coeurs* or hearts (representing the clergy), *carreaux* – arrowheads or diamonds (soldiers), *trèfles* or clubs (peasant farmers) and *piques* or spades (knights). Each suit was governed by its ruling family – the father (king), mother (queen) and male heir (knave or jack).

Some of these picture cards depicted history's best-known faces. Early kings appeared as Charlemagne (hearts), Julius Caesar (diamonds), Alexander the Great (clubs) and the biblical King David (spades). Popular queens were Joan of Arc, Helen of Troy and Elizabeth I.

Not content with visually reminding commoners of their place in society the nobles then invented rules to ram the message home. Early games such as gleek, pair and primero rewarded players for holding cards in groups such as runs, pairs and flushes. This was seen as more important than numerical supremacy, the point being that as long as humble fives mixed with other fives then everything would be dandy. Cards left without groups or partners were actively penalized, emphasizing their position as outcasts or outlaws.

DANGEROUS OBSESSIONS

Sociologists point to whist as a classic example of the way card games change to reflect social change. Original versions of this game rely on the turning of a card to choose trumps, an indication that social standing is a matter of fate that can't be challenged. But, later on, auction whist allows players to bid for the right to call trumps – or insist that there are none. Here the message is that any player with skill and bravery can impose him- or herself on others. A powerful single card, rather than a group, is now what counts.

Another factor that mitigated against medieval number games – or indeed fast play – was the design of suit patterns. Because these were highly intricate it was hard to tell at a glance whether you were holding, say, a nine or a ten of hearts. Although a few packs used Roman numerals, clear numbering didn't emerge until the Woolley Card Company printed some as an experiment in 1884. So if you were a successful medieval card counter you earned every groat of your winnings.

By the 17th century Europe was in the grip of gambling frenzy. Unending volumes of books on strategy were published, mathematics became the tavern-talk of odds-obsessed devotees and the aristocracy engaged card masters to school their children in etiquette and sound play. In the *Compleat Gamester* (1754) Richard Seymour cautions that 'he who, in company, should appear ignorant of the games in vogue would be reckoned low-bred and hardly fit for conversation'. Others were less convinced; Samuel Pepys dubbed cards 'this prophane, mad entertainment'.

In part the gambling love-in was driven by a new spirit of entrepreneurial adventure. The growth of the Lloyds shipping insurance market spread the idea of risk and reward, and vast profits promised from new markets in the colonies were hungrily eyed by men of means. Gambling tapped into this because it allowed everyone, from any social class, to stake money on a dream. The occasional high-profile disaster failed to deter people. Not even the South Sea Bubble.

In 1716 the South Sea Company was facing hard times. The slave market had proved unprofitable and slaves were inconsiderately dying in their hundreds during long voyages across the Atlantic. So a director of the company, John Blunt, hit on a plan already being tried in France in which the government would issue paper currency instead of gold. The paper had to carry a promise that it could be converted to gold (otherwise bankers would walk away) but once confidence was gained then the government could just print more notes any time it was strapped for cash.

Of course, we now know that this is complete tosh. Printing money willy-nilly causes inflation and economic disaster. But Blunt's offer to take on England's entire national debt (£50 million/$75 million) and pay £8 million ($12 million) for the privilege seemed a sure-fire winner. Anyone with, say, £1,000 in government bonds could cash them in at the usual miserly rate of interest or re-invest in South Sea shares with a promise of huge returns.

Each share would have an initial value of £100 and so an £1,000 investor would get ten for his money. But if there were more buyers than shares available (and the hype Blunt generated ensured there were) then the price would inevitably rise, perhaps to £200. Now the £1,000 investor was entitled to only five shares, giving the South Sea company an instant paper profit of £1,000. As long as the share price kept rising, investors kept stepping up.

To gambling-mad England it seemed a certain bet. Widows threw in their life savings, farm workers borrowed from wealthier friends and the upper classes liquidated assets to ensure a maximum stake. No one seemed bothered that the South Sea Company wasn't actually *doing* anything productive. Soon dozens of other speculators were offering stock in perpetual-motion devices, anti-pirate ships or silkworm farms – all with the promise of fabulous rewards.

One entrepreneur pocketed £2,000 ($3,000) on his first day in business after promoting a company with the aim of 'carrying on an undertaking of great advantage but no one to know what it is'. The great advantage turned out to be his and he vanished the same evening.

In the end, Blunt's greed was his undoing. He prosecuted four of his biggest rivals, who didn't possess the required royal charter. The courts backed him and all four went bust. To pay their debts the directors sold their most valuable assets which, naturally, were South Sea Company shares. Soon word spread that big names were cashing in and market sentiment moved like lightning. South Sea stock crashed literally overnight and investors like the Duke of Chandos lost £300,000 ($450,000) in a matter of days.

In the uproar that followed, Blunt was hauled before Parliament to have his personal fortune confiscated. Yet those who had sold early enough *did* make money. The 'Bubble' was seen by many as just another glorified gamble.

If the 'Bubble' was bizarre, one-to-one betting among the upper classes became downright barmy. The 18th century saw some truly Pythonesque examples – riding backwards on a horse from London

> '[Gambling is] the apparent desire to accept the certainty of losing money in the long run in return for the remote possibility of winning it in the short.' Bernard Levin

to Edinburgh, walking to Constantinople and back in a year and, most famously, a wager by the Counte d'Artois with Marie Antoinette that he could build the Bagatelle Palace in six weeks. Yet not all aristocrats regarded gambling as an eccentric distraction. The Marquis de Dangeau, for instance, ruthlessly played cards to win – unsportingly calculating probability and averages in every hand he held. It made him unpopular but rich.

By now gambling in Europe was becoming an industry. Private London clubs such as Whites, Crockfords and Almack's (later Brooks's) outwardly cultivated respectability with strict dress codes and etiquette, but once inside the toff-about-town could look forward to free wine, meals, music and dancing as an enticement to play the gaming tables. Private bets were usually overseen by the management although spur-of-the-moment propositions were not always policed.

According to one story, attributed to the writer and MP Horace Walpole, a gambler collapsed at Almack's, inadvertently creating a market in his survival prospects. Bets were taken for and against his chances with those 'selling' the man's life complaining bitterly at 'cheating' attempts to revive him. The man apparently died but history doesn't tell us whether there was an inquest or a steward's inquiry.

SATANIC VICES

The obsession of the educated classes with gambling is neatly illustrated in John Ashton's *The History Of Gambling In England* (New York, 1869). Referring to the MP Charles James Fox (who founded Brooks's with Walpole in 1764) Ashton writes, 'He had sat up playing Hazard, at Almack's, from Tuesday evening the fourth until five in the afternoon of Wednesday the fifth. On Thursday he spoke in the debate, went to dinner at half-past eleven at night; from thence to White's where he drank until seven the next morning; thence to Almack's, where he won £6,000; and between three and four in the afternoon he set out for Newmarket.' For privileged men like this, gambling was a reason for existing. Social lives were built around it and the exclusivity it bestowed.

For the poor things were rather different. As we've already seen, rulers and bishops had for centuries tried to clamp down on the 'Satanic vice' of lower-class gambling, and the Reformation gave Protestant leaders a chance to really put the boot it. It was seen as a travesty of God's natural laws because it allowed wealth to be acquired not from hard work and thrift but through luck. It also encouraged a blasphemous desire for material gain, wasted time and encouraged idleness.

Although this attitude eased during the Restoration and the printing boom the gambling nobility soon found new ways to stop the poor gatecrashing their show. First they taxed gaming implements – sixpence on a pack of cards; five shillings on a pair of dice – then they passed new laws banning specific games such as Hazard, Bassett, Faro and Ace of Hearts from public gaming houses, or *hells* as they were known. Royal palaces, and anywhere approved by the monarch, such as gentlemen's private clubs, were of course exempt from the legislation.

Inevitably, gambling was driven underground into the grateful arms of conmen and card sharps. Illegal gaming taverns were set up in safe houses, modified to include secret passages, escape routes and spyholes. The gaming room itself was concealed in the heart of the building, an inner sanctum open only to the initiated. All this told the unwary visitor that gambling was exciting, daring and adventurous; a brotherhood for the ordinary man. In reality the hells were appropriately named. The décor was a world away from Whites or Crockfords and the clientele included many a 'verser' or 'taker-up' – underworld speak for a card sharp – who preyed on 'cousins' (victims).

LOTTERY BOOMTIME

The result of anti-gaming law was that the poor turned in their droves to lotteries. These were hardly revolutionary in concept. Roman emperors had been fond of scattering prize tickets among spectators at the Games, and when fire destroyed much of Nero's Rome, lotteries helped to rebuild it. In the early 15th century the burghers of Burgundy and Sluis, Holland, used local draws to bankroll fortifications and by the mid-16th-century Italian cities such as Milan, Venice, Turin and Florence had government-approved lottery monopolies.

Around this time the French and Germans introduced national lotteries, an idea that to the fragile states of Europe seemed heaven sent. Why risk unpopularity through taxes when you could gently and regularly fleece the people via a lottery? In fact there were occasional difficulties with heaven via its earthly representatives. Some bishops retained their suspicions about pagan practices and occasional bouts of anti-lottery law were needed to mollify them and their fellow moralizers.

Even so, Pope Sixtus V blessed a French lottery in which losing tickets carried the slogan 'God Comforts You' and winning ones read 'God Has Chosen You'. This moral flexibility was emphasized by the Vatican's Lottery of the Roman States in 1732, part of a long and not-so-proud tradition of boosting papal coffers by whatever means. This was indeed the same Church that curtailed its criticism of Spain's cocaine profits in South America after taking a cut of the profits (see *This Is Cocaine* also published by Sanctuary, 2002).

England provides the finest historical example of state ambivalence towards lotteries. The country's first public draw was held in 1569, an attempt by Elizabeth I's government to raise money both for the country's much-neglected infrastructure and for its colonial ambitions. Top prize was £5,000 ($8,000) and the draw carried the kind of imaginative USP you just don't see in today's marketing industry. Elizabeth's wheeze was to give a seven-day amnesty to all criminals, unless their actions were really heinous, who bought a ticket.

Unsurprisingly, it worked a dream. At home naval ports were upgraded, Westminster Bridge was built, water mains pipes laid and the first public libraries opened. Abroad it financed a push into the New World, financing the first English settlement in North America at Jamestown, Virginia.

By the end of the 17th century English lotteries were raising a massive £1.5 million ($2.25 million) a year. The aristocracy fuelled this bonanza on the basis that it was one's patriotic duty to swell the Treasury's coffers (although actually winning would have been uncouth). Despite its success the entire shooting match was halted by William of Orange's government in 1699 on the basis that lotteries were a 'common and publick nuisance' that caused 'excitement'. The precise reasoning is unclear but seems to come back to a mixture of good old-fashioned English snobbery and Puritanism.

Frankly, for the upper classes it was an outrage that the very poor could become very rich through the very simple purchase of a lottery ticket. What was the point in having a class system? The poor were there to work long and hard without grumbling, not go round dreaming excitedly of a better life.

Sure enough, when Queen Anne re-introduced a state lottery in 1709 there was a catch. At £10 ($15) a go it was beyond the reach of the masses, who were left to buy into unregulated private draws. Eleven years later even these were outlawed and private lotteries were effectively handed to the criminal fraternity. It wasn't until the early 19th century that a parliamentary committee took a fresh look at the whole lottery issue, concluding that it was 'radically vicious'. In 1826 the British lottery was finally put to rest until, 168 years later, it was rudely awakened by Camelot.

SPORT OF KINGS

The notion of gambling as gentlemen's business also permeated horseracing. This was partly a historical hangover from the chariot contests patronized by Assyrian and Roman rulers but it was the cost of keeping horses that really slammed the door on the lower classes. By the 12th century AD, racing in Britain was conducted by noblemen, riding their own horses, in their own grounds. King Charles II – the 'Father of the British Turf' – introduced basic rules along with specialist jockeys, and his enthusiasm was matched by that of his immediate successors, James II and Queen Anne. Both followed Charles's lead by building country lodges at Newmarket racetrack.

To the dismay of the monarchy, this exclusive little club was not to last. By the mid-18th century the press had tapped into popular sentiments by printing racecards, form guides, advance odds and a results service. Leisure time was evolving from the long country festivals dictated by the seasons to more rigid work/leisure patterns demanded by industry. Racing responded to this by making itself more accessible. More than a hundred towns now held regular meetings and, once again, it proved all too much for Parliament.

In 1740 MPs passed an Act that made any race illegal unless it carried an entrance fee and a minimum £50 ($75) prize. They also limited the most common, two-horse races, to Black Hambleton and Newmarket. The reasoning? That 'the Great Number of Horse Races for small Plates, Prizes or Sums of Money have contributed very much to the encouragement of idleness to the Impoverishment of the meaner sorts of the subjects of the Kingdom'. Put simply, this meant that the dog-idle poor couldn't be trusted to have a bet. But time was running out for the aristocratic racegoer. Capitalism cared little for class boundaries.

The advent of the railways, telegraph network, credit facilities and commercial bookmaking ensured that the racing industry got a firm foothold in Britain's high streets. More than 400 'betting houses' opened between 1847 and 1850, and their runners and agents became a ubiquitous feature of working-class culture. Parliament had another go at banning it all via the Street Betting Acts of 1853, 1874, 1892 and 1906 but this was merely whistling in the wind. The underworld took over, operating books with little interference from the authorities.

The Industrial Revolution and Thomas Cook's promotion of tourism inevitably brought with it new gambling pleasure zones. For the British aristocracy this meant visits to the fashionable European casinos springing up in Monaco, Hesse-Homburg, Nice and Cannes. Here popular attractions were craps, vingt-et-un (the ancestor of blackjack), baccarat and roulette.

Roulette possibly evolved from an older game known as EO (even-odd) in which a ball was spun around a wheel containing 40 pockets marked E and O. Players backed the ball to land either in the E or the O. You can see why it never really took off.

Europe's first legal casino opened at the Palais Royale, Paris, in 1808 with the personal approval of the Emperor Napoleon. Dozens of others soon appeared and between 1819 and 1837 the government emerged as the biggest winner, taking 137 million francs (£14.6 million) in tax from Parisian gaming houses alone. In his book *Gambling In Revolutionary Paris*, Russell T Barnhart describes a visit to the Palais:

> ...*you could see actors, dwarves, giants, ventriloquists, dancing dogs, puppets, quack doctors, mountebanks [conmen], pornographers, an orchestra of blind musicians and a restaurant...you have the highest class courtesans who have rooms upstairs – it was the nicest place in town.*

Bearing in mind that British casinos have only recently started serving beer and sandwiches you have to acknowledge the Palais' sheer style. Not even in Las Vegas can you chill out among dancing dogs, giants, quack doctors and pornographers.

What destroyed the Palais was the greed of neighbouring shops and restaurants. Proprietors suspected casinos of sucking away customer spending power. They campaigned for closure, the restored royalist government obliged and four casinos at the Palais were shut down amid a near riot on 31 December 1837. At least the shop owners got their come-uppance. Without the attractions of the casino the Palais district soon resembled a ghost town.

GRAND CASINO

Once again, we see a government trying and failing to control the market. Did Parisian casino owners shrug their shoulders, accept the state's wisdom and become croissant makers instead? Er, no, actually. They moved their businesses to independent duchies like Baden Baden and Luxembourg, which duly hit the jackpot in terms of economic growth. Perhaps the most successful venture was pioneered by the Blanc brothers, François and Louis, who in 1842 established the Kursaal gaming house in Hesse-Homburg.

According to an 1868 account in the London *Daily News*, François Blanc persuaded the Homburg prime minister to let him set up a roulette table in a private room at the Eagle Inn 'where a few German families stayed in the summer to drink the mineral waters and live cheaply'. After a successful summer Blanc was awarded an exclusive concession to build the Kursaal, which for 30 years would be the world's most famous casino. He paid $16,000 (£10,600) into the Homburg Treasury, laid out public gardens, paved the streets and installed gas lighting. The *Daily News* adds: 'Now, in 1868, the surrounding hills have numerous villas. There are more than four hundred and fifty acres of gardens, 10,000 annual visitors, twenty hotels and a hundred furnished houses.'

Unfortunately for Blanc the Kursaal was on borrowed time. Prussia's defeat of Austria in 1866 allowed it to annexe several independent duchies and on New Year's Eve 1872 the Prussians closed all remaining casinos. Having twice seen successful businesses shut by power-mad rulers you'd have thought Blanc would have taken the hint. Instead he spotted yet another new opportunity, this time in a remote, impoverished principality covering just eight square miles (20.7sq km) of France's southeast coastline. It was the start of a gambling legend – the Grand Casino de Monte Carlo, Monaco.

Blanc's move into Monaco turned it into the undisputed international playground of the rich. He avoided interference by giving the Principality a cut of the profits through a company called the Société des Bains de Mer, which is still in existence today. At the height of its fame the Grand Casino was entertaining 10,000 visitors a day and hosting the great and the good from across Europe. Regulars at the tables included British Prime Minister William Gladstone, Edward Prince of Wales (later King Edward VII) and a young politician called Winston Churchill, who in 1910 walked away with winnings of $780 (£520). Yet perhaps the most famous Monaco gambler of all was a Victorian engineer called Charles Jaggers, the man who broke the bank at Monte Carlo.

Before recounting Jaggers' story, it's worth outlining the odds of roulette. There are obviously many types of bet (odd or even, red or black, blocks, columns etc), but in Jaggers' case what mattered were stakes on the individual numbers from zero to 36.

On these the bank pays out at 35 to 1 and returns a winning player's stake money, a total of £36 ($54) on an initial stake of £1. Given that, with the zero, there are 37 numbers on the wheel we know from our laws of large numbers, average and probability, that in the very long term, we'd need to bet £1 every 37 separate spins to win £36. This produces a slight house margin of plus 2.7 per cent, a profit the casino will *always* win unless someone is cheating or the equipment is faulty.

BIASED WHEELS

Jaggers knew that in the 19th century it was quite hard to engineer a perfect, totally unbiased roulette wheel. The slightest imperfection, over many spins, would direct the ball more often to certain sections of the wheel. So he hired six accomplices who spent a month recording winning numbers on the Grand Casino's tables. Back in his hotel he noted a clear pattern emerging.

Jaggers then began a marathon session of roulette, playing only the biased wheels. His strategy was breathtakingly simple; back numbers in the favoured zones and wait for the law of large numbers to do the rest. He lost on countless spins but effectively he had turned the casino's precarious margin in his favour. As long as his stakes were sensibly managed (to guard against freak runs) the more he played the less likely he was to lose overall. And he didn't.

By the time the Grand Casino realized something was up Jaggers had won a staggering 1.5 million francs (£160,000). The biased wheels were all replaced and exhaustively tested and Monte Carlo moved on, poorer but wiser. Yet there were plenty more sharp gamblers born in the Jaggers mould.

In 1904 a 35-year-old American called William Darnborough turned up in Monte Carlo and astounded the tables with his staking technique. Darnborough would wait until the croupier had spun the ball and then place chips at lightning speed with both hands. One winning run netted him £83,000 ($124,500) that year and, according to the Reuters news agency, he was still winning six years later. 'Mr Darnborough leaves Monte Carlo for London today with winnings of £64,000 from one month's stay. He began with a capital of £1,200. He won up to £93,000 at his peak. He won from £12,000 to £16,000 a day. He left feeling his luck was at an end' (14 December 1910).

Three years later a Monte Carlo regular, CN Williamson, wrote in *McClure*'s magazine:

> *The greatest sensation of modern days has been made for several seasons running by an American – young clean-shaven, keen-eyed, pale-faced...when he won vast sums he did not smile; when he lost his expression never changed. His play was on numbers but seemed to vary from time to time, occasionally being for 'repeats', often skipping from one side of the wheel to the other. No one could understand what he was doing, though it was evident he had a system of some sort as he staked without hesitation. The American often lost but his wins were immensely higher than his losses.*

Serious roulette players have argued for years over Darnborough's strategy. To win as he did almost certainly required some kind of system but there is still no truly plausible explanation. Williamson suspected he had an accomplice who 'signalled at the last moment' to predict the quarter of the wheel in which the ball would land. In his book, *The Money-Spinners*, Jacques Black argues that Darnborough devised a way of analyzing the position of the croupier's hand and the speed at which he spun the ball. Neither of these explanations quite cuts the mustard.

SCIENTIFIC EDGE

Gambling's greatest mathematical brain, Edward Thorp, spent years trying to predict the path of a roulette ball. He threw everything into the equation; the speed of the central rotor, the entry point and velocity of the ball, the tilt of the wheel, the bounce and scatter effects of hitting the number cups, and the effects of friction. He concluded that no croupier had a predictable enough spinning technique to offer the player a worthwhile edge.

If he had found a winning roulette system Thorp, a maths professor at the University College of Los Angeles, would have been happy to share it. In 1962 his epoch-making book *Beat The Dealer* sent shockwaves through the casino business because it offered a mathematically proven way to achieve up to a 2 per cent advantage over the house at blackjack. Thorp showed that because played hands are not returned to the pack after a round of blackjack (to save time shuffling) even a rookie card counter could work out roughly the shape of subsequent hands.

He also realized that some cards (not necessarily the pictures) favoured the player over the dealer. When an undealt deck held a large enough proportion of these cards, that was the time to bet and bet big. Over a long game the dealer would win more *hands* than the player. But the player would win more *money* by betting larger amounts on the juiciest decks.

The casinos, quite rightly, regarded Thorp's book as dangerous knowledge. They responded by keeping up to six packs in play at any one time and instructing croupiers to avoid dealing to the bottom. This proved an effective counter to Thorp's system but for the gaming rooms there was another unexpected bonus. Thousands of punters flocked to the Nevada tables carrying well-thumbed volumes of *Beat The Dealer*. Unfortunately, few had the basic playing skills or card-counting memory required to win even under the old etiquette of play. Nevada casinos rang up record profits.

HI-TECH CHEATS

However much the casino managements disliked Thorp's system, they couldn't label it cheating. Cheats did however adapt his roulette research, most notably a motley collection of scientists, gamblers and computer nerds who called themselves Eudaemonic Enterprises. They developed a James Bond-style arrangement in which a computer was concealed in a player's shoe. Ball and rotor speeds were measured by tapping the shoe every time the ball passed a specific point and a program analyzed which group of five numbers was most likely to win. This data was transmitted electronically to the bettor. Unlikely though it sounds, the scheme worked well under laboratory conditions. The problem arose when background electronic 'clutter' in the casino affected the team's delicate communications system.

Eudaemonic was one gambling scam that failed. But there are plenty of historical examples that were wonderfully conceived and executed. There isn't the space here to do justice to them all but any punter who has ever been mugged by the bookies should take heart from the tale of the Trodmore Race Club. It proves beyond doubt that there is a God and that he doesn't like bookmakers.

In July 1898 the London racing paper *The Sportsman* received a letter on expensive headed notepaper announcing that the Trodmore Race Club of Trodmore, Cornwall, planned to hold its first ever National Hunt meeting on the forthcoming bank holiday, Monday 1 August. The Clerk of the Course, one C Martin, gave full particulars and promised an official racecard would follow in the post.

There was nothing unusual about this. In Victorian Britain National Hunt racing was a disorganized business and dozens of obscure country meetings cropped up all over the place, especially on bank holidays. The editors of *The Sportsman* were more concerned about how they would get the results and starting prices.

As luck would have it, a letter landed on the racing desk some days later from a gentleman who would be in Cornwall on the 1st and planned to attend Trodmore. With so many meetings that day, might *The Sportsman* need a little assistance? For a small fee, he would wire the results and SPs up to the newspaper for publication the following day. The deal was struck, the racecard arrived and on the morning of 1 August it duly appeared in the paper.

Across London that morning, street bookmakers did a lot of business on the Trodmore meeting. A few queried the location but the punters always had a newspaper racecard to show them. The bookies shrugged and took the money. If it was good enough for a respected organ such as *The Sportsman* it was good enough for them.

You will by now have spotted the sting. There was of course no such place as Trodmore. The letters to *The Sportsman* were from a syndicate of gambling fraudsters who had made up the runners and riders. They also picked the results of the non-existent races and fixed the starting prices. A couple of 'winners' romped home at satisfyingly long odds of 5-1, while others were apparently well backed – Jim (5-4), Curfew (6-4), Fairy Bells (7-4) and Spur (2-1). All fairly unremarkable. The following day bookies began paying out.

But not all bookies. Some wanted to check the starting prices in *The Sportsman*'s rival paper the *Sporting Life* and, when none could be found, decided to make further inquiries. In the meantime the *Life*, which had not been given the 'official' results by the syndicate, decided to copy them anyway in its 3 August edition. In doing so a sub-editor or printer made the mistake of quoting one long-odds winner, appropriately named Reaper, at 5-2 rather than 5-1. This was enough for the bookies who began checking maps of Cornwall. Shortly afterwards they called the police.

No one was ever caught for the Trodmore scam. Neither do we know how much the syndicate made. Suspicion was heavily focused on a group of Fleet Street journalists but there was never enough evidence to mount a prosecution. It makes you laugh, doesn't it, to think of punters placing bets when they already know the result.

Couldn't happen now of course. Certainly not at one of the world's most prestigious, richest and best-known races with all the safeguards provided by computerized security. Or could it? Well, check out the Breeders Cup Pick Six Scandal in the Money chapter (see p178).

THAT'S LOLLAPALOOZA

One last thing to remember about betting frauds: they don't always need the meticulous attention to detail deployed by the Trodmore team. Sometimes you get stung because you fail to check a gambling fundamental. Namely, Know The Local Rules.

The best illustration of this appeared in John Lillard's *Poker Stories*, written around 1896. The story, titled *The Lollapalooza*, is précised below. Who cares whether it's true...

A professional card sharp breezes into a remote Montana town to have some fun fleecing the locals at poker. They play a few straight hands until he deals himself the usual four aces and ups the stake money. After several rounds of betting only one player has stayed with him: a canny, elderly gold prospector. The sharp keeps betting until he sees all the old-timer's chips in the pot. Then he flicks over his aces, smiles down at his opponent's worthless concoction of clubs and diamonds and reaches out for the winnings.

But the old guy is still smiling. 'Friend,' he says, 'in this town a Lollapalooza beats all at poker. And those there clubs and diamonds – that's a Lollapalooza.' The disbelieving sharp gazes round the table to see a series of nodding heads. Nothing, they agree, beats a Lollapalooza.

Determined to recoup his losses the furious visitor waits a couple of hands before dealing himself exactly the same selection of clubs and diamonds. Up goes the betting and again the old-timer stays with him. Finally, with a flourish and broad grin, the sharp reveals his 'unbeatable' Lollapalooza and leans forward to take the pot. Only then does he notice his rival has a pair of kings and is *still* smiling.

'Friend,' says the greybeard, 'shoulda checked the local rules 'fore you started. In this town, the ol' Lollapalooza can only ever be played once a night.'

Which takes us nicely into the Wild West.

GAMBLING IN THE NEW WORLD
Once lotteries had helped build England's first permanent American colony at Jamestown they became a pillar of the fledgling New World economy. Over the years state draws financed the War of Independence, supported national universities like Harvard and bankrolled major public projects. Unfortunately the system also bred bureaucrats, middle men and fraudsters, a problem neatly illustrated in 1811 by the launch of the Commonwealth of Pennsylvania's lottery to pay for a $340,000 (£230,000) Union Canal. Some years this netted an astonishing $6,600,000 (£4,400,000), of which barely $30,000 (£20,000) actually reached the Union Canal Company.

Yet as the 19th century wore on politicians fell back into the Puritan groove. In 1827 Congress forbade postmasters from acting as lottery agents, in 1868 all lottery material was banned from the mail and by 1890 it was illegal to mail any newspaper that carried a lottery ad. The federal government clearly felt it had to save the people from themselves and, incredibly, the Land of the Free was still banning adverts for state lotteries as late as 1975.

For serious gamblers none of this mattered a dime. They didn't much care for the stingy odds and clinical procedures of the lottery, especially when there was a tense, tactical, intelligent, skilful and potentially far more lucrative game played in every two-bit town with a saloon bar since the heyday of the Wild West. Gradually, poker became woven into the DNA of all but the most God-fearing families.

> According to Wild West poker folklore a man suspected of cheating found his hand pinned to the table by a knife. 'My friend,' said his opponent, 'if the queen of spades is not under your hand then I owe you an apology.'

It's not clear where or when poker was invented. Most likely the rules were bolted together from earlier card games such as the French *poque* or German *pochspiel*, both of which were played in the 18th century. In 1834 the American writer Jonathan H Green mentions what he calls the 'cheating game' of poker, popular on Mississippi riverboats. He only later realized that it was not listed in *Hoyles*, the rules bible for all card enthusiasts, and was effectively a new gambling cult.

Poker soon became synonymous with gunslingers, specifically the characters featured below. None of them had terribly liberal attitudes to (a) losing and (b) cheating so unless you were a natural-born loser, an accomplished card sharp or a real-life ringer for Alan Ladd in *Shane* it was usually best to sit outside with a glass of buttermilk.

JAMES 'WILD BILL' HICKOK

Born at Troy Grove, Illinois, in 1837 Hickok honed his shooting skills in childhood, which just goes to show what a kid can do without the modern distractions of TV and computers.

By the age of 18 he was drifting west, working variously as a hired gun, stagecoach driver and farmhand. After serving as a Union scout in the Civil War he became a US marshal in some of the West's toughest towns – acquiring living legend status in the process. Pulp fiction writers relished his reputation as a gambler, womanizer (he supposedly seduced Martha

'Calamity Jane' Burke) and fighter, and he took advantage of this free PR by going into showbusiness. He starred as 'Wild Bill' in a play called *Scouts Of The Prairies* and, in 1872, began a two-year tour of the eastern states with Buffalo Bill Cody's Wild West Show.

By 1876 he was back on the frontier and gambling as hard as ever. That year he was shot in the back of the head while playing poker at a saloon in Deadwood. The hand he held – two pairs, aces over eights – has since passed into gambling folklore as the 'Dead Man's Hand'.

WYATT EARP

Another Illinois kid, Wyatt Berry Stapp Earp, carved his livelihood from whatever came along. He was a professional card player, bison hunter, stagecoach driver and railway construction worker, but his outstanding skill was fist-fighting. His punching ability earned him the nickname 'the Earp Ape' from brothers James and Virgil.

In 1876, aged 28, Wyatt Earp became chief deputy marshal of Dodge City. A year later he took his law enforcement skills to Deadwood and by 1879 had settled in Tombstone, Arizona, becoming Deputy US Marshal for the entire territory. His finest hour came in 1881 when, together with Doc Holliday and three of his brothers, he killed several cattle rustlers in the Gunfight at the OK Corral. He died in Los Angeles in 1929.

DOC HOLLIDAY

Born in Georgia 1852 John Henry Holliday trained as a dentist but spent most of his working life as a professional gambler. On medical advice (he suffered from tuberculosis) he moved to the warmer climes of Dallas, Texas, in the 1870s and soon found work as a faro dealer. At various times he gambled his way around the mining camps of Central City, Idaho Springs, Georgetown and Boulder.

It was never a quiet life. Doc Holliday was rarely without his pistol or knife, and his hot temper got him involved in eight shootings and numerous stabbings. He died in Glenwood Springs, Colorado, in 1883, ten minutes after drinking his morning whisky. His last words – 'this is funny' – supposedly reflected his surprise at dying from natural causes.

BAT MASTERSON

Another Illinois bad boy, William Barclay Masterson was born in 1855, moving to Denver, Colorado, in 1890. There he found work at the Palace Theater as house gambler and manager of the resident troupe of dancing girls.

Within two years he was managing a bar and gambling den in Creede – one of Colorado's roughest mining towns – and became the local marshal. His reputation as a gunslinger ensured his presence was usually enough to stifle trouble.

Masterson ended his days as sports editor on the New York *Morning Telegraph*. He died working at the paper's offices in 1921.

POKER ALICE

Though not strictly speaking a gunfighter, Alice Duffield packed a six-shooter and was a match for any man at the poker tables. The daughter of a schoolmaster, she was born in Sudbury, Suffolk, England, in 1851, emigrating to America when she was 12. She married engineer Frank Duffield in Colorado seven years later but was soon widowed after a mining accident.

Alice shunned a career in teaching and got herself hired as a poker dealer. She was working for Bob Ford (the 'dirty little coward' who shot Jesse James) when Ford was himself gunned down by a gambler at his Creede saloon. Alice then headed for Deadwood where she fell in love with fellow poker player William Tubbs, a man she saved from a drunken, knife-wielding miner who had accused him of cheating. Poker Alice shot the miner in the arm. She was not a woman to cross.

Sadly Tubbs died from pneumonia and Alice had to pawn her engagement ring to get him buried. She got the ring back after winning big in a poker game and by 1912 was running a successful gaming club at Fort Meade, South Dakota. She never gave up the big cigars she'd smoked all her life and died of cancer aged 78.

MOB HANDS

By the early 20th century commercial gambling was banned in most American states. Mafia moguls had long operated illegal casinos but the end of Prohibition in 1933 gave them a new incentive. With bootlegging profits wiped out, a new income stream was needed. Gambling fitted nicely into the Mob's business portfolio, alongside prostitution and protection.

One of the best-known dens could be found at the magnificent Floridian Hotel, Miami Beach, an operation set up in 1929 by a big-money gambler from North Carolina called Arthur Childers. Childers teamed up with the wealthy Detroit gaming tycoon Bert Moss and together they set about protecting their investment. Moss ran the 'security' while Childers used his influence as a Miami Beach councilman to keep the cops away.

Visiting gamblers would find themselves ushered into an elevator for a ride to the ninth floor. From here they were taken up some stairs and into a guest room where staff would check their credentials and direct them into what looked like the toilet. It was actually the casino entrance.

Unfortunately for Childers and Moss the Floridian became a victim of its own success. Al Capone and another godfather, St Louis Dutch, muscled in on the action and their involvement attracted the unwelcome attentions of J Edgar Hoover's FBI and the Internal Revenue Service. The Mafia was discovering that underworld casinos were vulnerable beasts. The alternative was simple. Go legal.

BUGSY'S VEGAS

At the end of World War II Las Vegas was an unremarkable town in the middle of the Nevada desert. There were a few dude ranches and resort hotels for the tourists but Vegas didn't do mass market. It was an 18-hour flight from the East Coast, the rail link was primitive and in high summer the drive from Los Angeles was like a sauna on wheels. Adventurous types who tried it sometimes found bits of their car melting.

Despite all this Las Vegas had a precious asset. It lay in Nevada, the only state offering legal gambling. Legislators had tried the idea during the Depression as a way of bringing in investment and in the 1940s they expanded it further to allow off-track betting on horse races. The war years hadn't exactly been boom time, although there were a couple of upmarket casinos in the north around Reno. Las Vegas was still virgin territory for gambling and a 'businessman' from back east liked what he saw. His name was Benjamin Siegelbaum, better known as Bugsy Siegel.

Siegel's life of crime dates back to his early days in Brooklyn where he ran extortion and protection rackets. There he teamed up with two other hoods who would become Mafia legends, Meyer Lansky and Charlie 'Lucky' Luciano, and it was to them he turned for the funds to build his gambling mecca in Vegas. Siegel had some experience running floating casinos (legal because they traded outside US territorial waters). But his plans for the Flamingo Hotel were on an altogether different scale. Other Mob leaders who'd tested the water with modest Nevada operations moved quickly to back him.

It all started so well. Siegel bought a controlling stake in the Flamingo after the original developer, Billy Wilkerson, ran out of cash. The décor was outrageous, tiled bathrooms and air conditioners were standard in all rooms and there were two swimming pools in which gamblers could chill out. Best of all, Siegel could whistle up his movie star pals for a coast-to-coast press launch.

And yet by December 1946, a year after construction began, the godfathers had not seen a dollar's profit. Post-war building materials were expensive and the Mafia-infested Teamsters' Union was rumoured to be fleecing Bugsy through a range of scams. One such was the 'Palm Tree Shuttle', in which the same trees were hauled to and from California and sold to the Flamingo several times over.

With the original $1.2 million (£0.8 million) estimate for the hotel now topping $6 million (£4 million), the Syndicate was in an ugly mood. A summit meeting was called in Cuba where Lansky sensationally claimed his old pal Bugsy was skimming the budget. Reluctantly, he advised fellow mobsters to take out a contract with the proviso that Siegel's execution be delayed until after the Flamingo casino opened on 27 December. If all went well, Bugsy could be squeezed to pay back his dues. If it flopped...hitman Charlie Fischetti would blow him away.

Siegel knew none of this but he was doing all he could. More than 40 big Hollywood names attended the Flamingo launch, including Clark Gable, Lana Turner, Caesar Romero, Joan Crawford and Anne Jeffreys.

The stage show was spectacular; the champagne came in fountains and, in the words of legendary Vegas gambler Benny Binion, it was 'the biggest whoop-de-do I ever seen'. But because none of the hotel rooms was finished, celebrity guests soon took their money back to LA. Siegel kept the casino going for a couple more weeks but by mid-January it was closed pending completion of the hotel.

Bugsy was now on death row although Lansky was still working overtime to keep him alive. Things looked hopeful when, in May 1947, just three months after the casino's re-launch, the hotel reported half-year profits of $250,000 (£16,500). Siegel seemed to be through the worst, and the evening of 20 June saw him relaxing at the Hollywood retreat he shared with his actress partner, Virginia Hill. She was in Switzerland after one of their habitual tiffs and he sat alone reading the papers.

> Mobster Meyer Lansky, who together with Bugsy Siegel and 'Lucky' Luciano controlled much of America's post-war gambling industry, was thought to be worth $400 million (£300 million) when he died of lung cancer in Miami Beach, Florida, on 15 May 1983.

At about 10.30pm eight bullets smashed through the window. One hit his head, taking out an eye. Four more slammed into his lungs. There was no doubt that he'd died instantly but, to this day, no one has properly answered the big question. Just who did shoot Bugsy Siegel?

Fischetti is the obvious answer although many commentators believe Lansky would never have sanctioned the hit. Perhaps more likely is that other members of the Syndicate, less burdened by the baggage of friendship, lost patience and arranged their own contract. Either way, the Flamingo outlived them all. It was later bought by a major chain and now has more than 3,500 rooms, making it one of the ten biggest hotels in the world.

THE BLACK BOOK

The influx of Mafia money to Vegas after World War II eventually spurred the Nevada Legislature to tighten its rules. In 1953 it ordered that gaming licences should be withheld from anyone guilty of a felony, narcotics, larceny or firearms violation within the previous five years.

In 1959 further reforms established the Gaming Control Board, an investigative organization, and the Nevada Gaming Commission, responsible for licences. To keep the Mafia on its toes Governor Grant Sawyer also created the *Nevada Black Book*, a list of undesirable individuals banned from gambling premises across the state. Among the first 11 names was one Sam 'Momo' Giancana, a leading Chicago mobster. In July 1963 he achieved worldwide notoriety in a scandal that threatened to destroy Ol' Blue Eyes himself, Frank Sinatra.

Sinatra owned the Cal Nevada Lodge, a casino at Lake Tahoe, and for a few days that month Giancana was booked into chalet No 50 with Phyllis McGuire of the singing McGuire Sisters. Phyllis was onstage most nights but had one Monday free and accompanied Giancana in a lodge car for dinner in Reno. On the ride back they ran out of fuel and stopped for help at the Christmas Tree Inn. There staff recognized the mobster, realized where he was staying and tipped off the GCB.

There could be no question that Cal Nevada employees knew who Giancana was, that he was in the *Black Book* and that he should never have been a guest. The implication was that Sinatra himself had cleared the booking. Matters were not helped when two gaming agents who were coincidentally checking the Lodge casino count reported that an employee had tried to bribe them.

In response a furious Sinatra did it his way and telephoned GCB chairman Ed Olsen who, according to newspaper reports, was 'maligned and vilified by the use of foul and repulsive language which was venomous to the extreme'. Soon afterwards Sinatra dropped his gaming licence for Cal Nevada – before it could be removed – and announced that his 'investments and interests were too diversified and that it would be in my best interests to devote most, if not all, of my time to the entertainment industry'.

LONDON MAFIA

With the Swinging '60s now well under way, Mafia-backed casinos began doing brisk business in London. In 1967 eight godfathers were banned from entering the UK on the basis that their presence was 'not conducive to the public good'. According to a report in the *Sunday Telegraph* of 3 March

1968 Mafia bosses were so concerned by new British gambling legislation that they held a 'crisis conference' in Miami. The summit was apparently chaired by Angelo Bruno, representing Meyer Lansky's East Coast Syndicate.

What most concerned the Americans was a line in the 1968 Gaming Act that banned anyone with a criminal record from holding a stake in a UK casino. They were right to be worried because this struck at the very heart of underworld gambling in London. The Act is admired even today by Metropolitan Police Vice Squad officers. Over at Salford University's Centre for Gambling Studies Dr Greg Anderson regards the Mafia's presence as a driving force behind this change. He explained:

> Before the 1960s there was essentially a prohibition culture surrounding gambling in the UK. Apart from on-course betting, credit betting and the football pools, gambling was prohibited.
>
> Then came some very specific legislation. In 1960 Parliament opened up off-course betting but also, because of a loophole in the law, created a proliferation of casinos and bingo halls. Bingo was not problematic but casinos needed another round of legislation in 1968 which basically tightened the law.
>
> It placed all kinds of demands on casino operators, some of which now look archaic but were actually the key to probity. For example you couldn't open a casino unless you could prove a demand which hadn't been met by current operators. You could only open in a town or city of a certain size – 125,000 people. You had to be a fit and proper person, you couldn't advertise, you couldn't serve alcohol and you couldn't offer entertainment. It was about as far away from Las Vegas as was possible to be.
>
> All these safeguards developed out of the proliferation of unlicensed casinos in the '60s and fears that they were being run by the American Mafia, which was partly true – particularly in London.

SLOTTING IN

Although gambling crime conjures up images of vast gangland networks it has historically been a happy hunting ground for small-time scamsters.

Mechanic Charles Fey's invention of the slot machine in 1887 was great news for them because once the mechanical processes had been understood it was relatively simple to manipulate payouts. Fey's machine was a primitive random-number indicator in which pulling a lever spun three reels bearing symbols such as cards, horses and pieces of fruit. Line up a winning combination and nickels would rain into the tray below.

The first slot scams were fairly primitive. They included 'stringing' (tying thin wire to a coin and drawing it back up), squirting in detergent cleaner and using counterfeit or foreign coins. But by the 1940s dedicated slots players had worked out a subtler technique. Like good Catholic women they practised the 'rhythm method', based on the knowledge that all reels revolved the same number of times per pull. By remembering the relative positions of all symbols it was possible to predict the next sequence.

Though useful in itself, the importance of this 'inside' information was magnified by a design flaw. When the reels stopped spinning it could take a second or so for the brake mechanism to disengage. If symbols were properly aligned, pulling the arm just before brake release could push them into a payout combination. In post-war Britain this became a much-admired skill among unemployed young men desperate for cash. You could even sign up for courses on the secrets of reel control. Understandably, slot manufacturers were less impressed and the introduction of spin variators in 1951 put an end to the fun.

American slot machines were exported all over the world but there was one country that embraced them like no other. Up until World War II, enterprising Australians had quietly supplemented their income by illegally operating slots in their back rooms at home. Occasionally, if there wasn't much else on, police would mount a raid and smash them up. Then, like so many other governments worldwide, state legislators in New South Wales turned the law on its head.

First, a little background. Australians have an obsession with gambling in general – and slot machines in particular – which is rooted in the very first days of the colony. Professor Jan McMillen, director of the Australian National University's Centre for Gambling Research in Canberra, sums it up with typical Aussie aplomb.

Australians love gambling full stop. We'll gamble on anything and historically our attitudes have been shaped very differently from Britain and the US. America was settled by Pilgrim Fathers escaping the immorality of Georgian England. They wanted a moral, upright, vice-free society and that meant no gambling. Australia was settled by accident, by the immoral people Georgian Society didn't want.

We were the rejects. We gambled in the hulks at Plymouth, we gambled on the voyage, we gambled when we got here and we've been gambling ever since. The first major public event in Australia was a race meeting organized by Governor [Lachlan] Macquarie to try and stop drunk and disorderly behaviour in the early colony. After that governments tended to legalize and legitimize gambling. There are some wonderful 19th-century documents upholding every man's right to gamble in Australia. This is a very different background to the US and UK.

The rise of the slot machine in Australia is another historical accident stemming back to the end of World War II when the country developed a vibrant economy built on migration from Europe and the return of its armed forces.

That period brought a lot of affluence. Drinking became a major problem. These guys had money to spare and particularly around NSW and Sydney the pubs were into a goldmine and alcohol consumption went through the roof. It was all very male dominated – women were absolutely forbidden from drinking in hotels; it was a real bloke's domain.

We had a policy called the six o'clock swill. I grew up in this period and I remember it well. A few minutes before the pubs closed at 6pm the blokes would line up six or seven drinks, down the lot, get pushed out the door, create disorder on the streets and then head home to beat up their wives.

There then came a move by some very progressive social policy reformers to civilize Australia's drinking habits. The slot machines

117

were it. They were allowed into social, football and golf clubs to create a revenue source so that clubs could provide meals for men and women to eat together in a civilized environment. It was a cash cow to end a social problem.

Of course, things didn't work out quite like that. Shame the scientists didn't know more about addiction.

Mind, they still don't know a lot.

> 'Gambling is a disease of barbarians, superficially civilized.'
>
> – WR Inge, Dean of St Paul's Cathedral, London

Can gambling be a disease? Can it be 'caught' like a germ? Is it something in people's genes? A psychiatric illness? Can someone's age or social standing make them vulnerable? Is it psychologically beneficial? Or can it kill? The answers to these questions are probably, possibly, perhaps, sometimes, could be, maybe and depends what you mean by 'kill'. We can safely conclude, therefore, that the causes, effects and treatment of compulsive gambling are among the most poorly understood areas in modern medicine.

Who's to blame for this morass? The media is, naturally, blamed for absolutely everything but in this case the charge has some substance. We journalists like our stories clear-cut, with proper heroes and villains. Don't start telling us gambling might be both a good and bad thing because we can't hack that kind of trendy thinking. Oh, and we also really like junk science surveys that allow sweeping conclusions with little basis in fact.

Politicians either downplay the health effects of gambling (especially if they're getting sponsorship from the gaming industry) or exaggerate its dangers (especially if their constituencies are packed with the religious right). The problem is not so much a lack of research as a lack of *conclusive* research. So we have a dial-a-study culture in which politicians can always dust down some figures somewhere to shore up a position. Given the conflicts of interest, political statements about gambling should carry compulsory health warnings.

Then there are the scientists who conduct research to support a pet theory, as if the theory must be right, and academics who come up with social models and definitions that become ingrained on a generation of students as shibboleths. While these are important as a basic framework for research, the idea that they are necessarily appropriate – or even right – has to be constantly challenged.

The truth is that, like alcohol or cocaine, gambling can and does destroy lives. It may also be beneficial and good fun. In trying to reconcile these two extremes we first need to look at the mechanics of problem gambling, addiction and the meaning of all those buzz-words that zoom around the research arena.

DEFINING THE PROBLEM

Two main screening systems are used to identify problem gambling. Firstly, there's the fourth revision of the *Diagnostic and Statistical Manual of Mental Disorders*, otherwise known as *DSM-IV*, which is produced by the American Psychiatric Association. This states that 'persistent and recurrent maladaptive gambling behaviour' is indicated by five or more of the following, summarized, symptoms:

A problem gambler...
1   *is preoccupied with past or planned gambling ventures and strategies.*
2   *needs to gamble with increasing amounts to achieve the desired excitement.*
3   *is repeatedly unsuccessful at curbing or stopping gambling.*
4   *is restless or irritable when attempting to cut down or stop.*
5   *gambles as a way of escaping problems or negative moods.*
6.   *chases losses.*
7   *lies to family members about the extent of gambling.*
8   *commits crimes such as forgery, fraud or theft to get gambling funds.*
9   *has lost or jeopardized a significant relationship, job or educational opportunity.*
10 *relies on others to provide money where gambling has caused a desperate financial situation.*

The second diagnostic method is the South Oaks Gambling Screen, or SOGS, produced in 1987 by Dr Henry Lesieur and Dr Sheila Blume. SOGS is a questionnaire that asks candidates about the type and frequency of their gambling, amounts wagered, family history, loss-chasing, personal perceptions, critical comments from friends or family, feelings of guilt, borrowings to pay gambling debt and concealment of betting slips or gambling 'slush funds'. Overall, SOGS is considered a better indicator of problem gambling although most psychologists believe the scoring formula has to be modified according to country and social context.

Defining the seriousness of an individual's gambling problem is inevitably subjective. Often researchers will use terms such as 'pathological' or 'compulsive' to describe gamblers with no control over their addiction. Then come 'problem' or 'disordered' gamblers for whom normal life is disrupted to various degrees. Dropping a further level we come to 'at risk' gamblers – people who regularly dabble but probably aren't hooked. Finally there are those who gamble infrequently or not at all. These broad definitions are usually categorized across three or four levels, with four being the most serious.

'At risk' is a particularly fuzzy notion. Are you at risk if you've ever gambled, even just the once? Does living near a casino or travelling to one put you in this category? This might sound like semantics but it is a crucially important definition in assessing the prevalence of problem gambling.

When epidemiologists talk of prevalence, they are dividing the number of people actually affected by a disease into the number at risk. The result is expressed as a percentage. Take the SARS virus, which provoked such worldwide panic in 2003. If 1,000 individuals have the disease and 100,000 in cities such as Toronto or Hong Kong are considered at risk then the prevalence rate is 1 per cent. But if ten million people in neighbouring cities and countries fall into the 'at risk' category then prevalence drops to 0.01 per cent. If the whole world is at risk, the prevalence based on 1,000 cases is too small to be meaningful.

The most comprehensive gambling research in recent times was conducted in 1999 by Chicago University's National Opinion Research Center (NORC) for America's National Gambling Impact Study Commission.

It concluded that between 0.1 and 0.6 per cent of the general adult population were pathological gamblers. This is a lower prevalence rate than that noted by the US National Research Council (0.9 per cent) and a 1997 Harvard Medical School analysis (1.29 per cent). The Harvard study pointed out that the prevalence of drug abuse/dependence (6.2 per cent) and alcohol dependence (13.8 per cent) was far higher.

These figures put the most extreme end of gambling addiction into some perspective. NORC estimated the total social costs of US problem and pathological gambling at $5-6 billion (around £4 billion) per year, a stark contrast to the $166 billion (£110 billion) bill for alcohol abuse and the $125 billion (£83 billion) cost of tackling heart disease.

The story in Britain is similar but not the same. According to the report *Gambling Behaviour In Britain*, published by the National Centre for Social Research in June 2000, the level of problem gambling among the country's adults was 0.8 per cent using the SOGS screen and 0.6 per cent using *DSM-IV*. However, these results are not directly comparable to those for the US because the British used more liberal interpretations of the model.

The survey threw up a few more interesting statistics, such as the UK male/female gambling divide. The following table shows the betting preferences of adult respondents expressed in percentages. Some 3,700 men and 3,900 women were questioned.

	Men	Women
National Lottery draw	68	62
Another lottery	9	8
Scratchcards	22	22
Football pools	13	5
Bingo	5	10
Fruit machines	20	8
Horseraces	18	9
Bookie bet – not dogs or horses	5	1
Table games in a casino	4	1
Private bets	17	6
Any gambling in past year	76	68

In Australia, as we've seen, the criteria for establishing problem gambling is, for cultural reasons, very different. Put another way, the Aussies have been gambling-crazy for years and would have pokies in their bathrooms given half the chance. According to the Victoria Casino and Gaming Authority report *Definition And Incidence Of Problem Gambling...* (July 2001), there is a prevalence rate of between 1 and 3 per cent of the adult population, depending on which state you survey. In reaching this figure Aussie rules were applied to the SOGS framework to make it meaningful within their gambling-mad culture.

In December 1999 the Australian Prime Minister, John Howard, issued his response to the country's Productivity Commission report. 'I am particularly disturbed,' he said, 'about the extent and severity of problem gambling. The report found that around 290,000 Australians are problem gamblers and account for over AUS$3 billion [£1.25 billion] in losses annually. This is disastrous not only for these problem gamblers but also for the estimated 1.5 million people they directly affect as a result of bankruptcy, divorce, suicide and lost time at work.'

Gambling's drain on public funds has become a hot political and public health issue. Over the last ten years both the Bush and Clinton administrations have threatened to target a gambler's winnings if he or she refuses to pay child support. Apart from the bureaucratic and privacy nightmare this would inflict on the gambling industry, it begs the obvious question: why stop at gambling? Why not tell banks to siphon off private funds to child support agencies? Why not freeze the dividends of stock market investors? Or stop new car buyers driving away?

Nevertheless, the industry does have to face the health and social problems it causes. A 1996 study *The Social Costs Of Gambling In Wisconsin* (Thompson, Gazel & Rickman) looked at four main categories – work-related (ie working hours lost to gambling, unemployment compensation, lost salaries), bad debts and theft costs, police and judicial costs (ie bankruptcy, cost of court proceedings and jail), and health and welfare costs (treatment, benefit payments etc). The total public bill from an estimated 32,425 problem gamblers was $307 million (£205 million) The cost in dollars per problem gambler worked out as shown here:

Health and welfare-related	695.49
Police and judicial-related	2,612.34
Work-related	2,940.89
Bad debt/theft-related	3,220.00
Total	9,468.72

Because so much gambling research emerges from America, it is natural to wonder how relevant it is to other cultures. Comparisons are complex and hard to interpret but the similarity of some results is striking. One study of indigenous peoples in North Dakota and New Zealand, for example, showed that both experienced much higher levels of problem gambling over a lifetime then their white neighbours. In the NZ analysis the figures were 5.9 per cent of Maoris compared to 1.7 per cent of Caucasians. In North Dakota it was 7.1 per cent of Native Americans compared to 0.8 per cent of Caucasians (Volberg & Abbott, 1997).

These figures confirmed an earlier study on reservations in the US Northern Plains that suggested Native Americans were more than twice as likely to become problem gamblers as were non-Native Americans (*A Comparative Study Of Problematic Gambling Behaviors*, D Zitzow, 1996). The difficulty is that the sample group was less educated, had lower income and more frequent histories of alcohol and marijuana use – all factors associated with pathological gambling. This suggests the results may have overestimated the risk to Native American communities.

Common sense dictates that problem gambling is at least partly attributable to the availability of casinos, betting shops, the Internet etc. So you'd think the opening of a new casino would show this. It's actually quite rare for a casino to start business in 'virgin' territory, but in 1999 a report in the *Journal of Gambling Studies* (Govoni, Frisch, Rupcich and Getty) looked at the before-and-after effects of the Casino Windsor in Ontario, Canada.

This study showed that, a year after the casino opened, levels of problem gambling actually fell among local men and women, and the number of compulsives increased by a statistically insignificant 0.5 per cent. Of course, a year may not be long enough to make a difference but the study does hammer home the need to challenge received wisdoms.

This is true particularly where the Internet is concerned. In the World chapter we looked at the sensational growth of net-bets and the supposed birth of an e-gambling junkie generation. Certainly, a study of 389 people (Ladd & Petry) in 2002 indicated that the number of pathological gamblers using the Internet outnumbered non-Internet compulsives by six to one. Sounds compelling doesn't it?

The way to get a sensible independent overview on gambling research is to log on to *The WAGER*, a weekly Internet newsletter produced by the Division on Addictions at Harvard Medical School. As far as possible, research is presented in layman's terms. Rarely is it reviewed uncritically but neither is it cynically trashed.

The WAGER points out that the Ladd & Petry study is both small and relies partly on 'self-selection', ie by leaving out questionnaires at university dental and health clinics. This suggests that at least some respondents took part because they liked gambling (they all had experience of it). Consequently the prevalence rate for problem gambling (26 per cent) was higher than for the general population, in which some people have never had a bet.

Also, there is the classic cause-and-effect problem. It may be that the Internet causes problem gambling. Then again, it may be that problem gamblers head for the Internet. You see the problem. *The WAGER's* verdict: interesting insight; larger random study required.

ACTION AND ESCAPE

Some researchers have tried to break down the most severe forms of compulsive gambling addiction into two distinct types – 'action' and 'escape' – each of which has four distinct phases. One of the most interesting papers on this has been written by Don Hulen and Paula Burns for the Arizona Council on Compulsive Gambling (ACCG). It is based largely on their personal observations over 40 years but they stress it doesn't necessarily relate to all pathological gamblers.

Hulen and Burns' work *Differences In Pathological Gamblers In Arizona*, last revised in February 2000, pulls no punches. It categorizes action gamblers as follows:

> *Action gamblers are usually domineering, controlling, manipulative men with large egos. They see themselves as friendly, sociable, gregarious and generous. Their average IQ is over 120. They are energetic, assertive, persuasive and confident. In spite of all this, they usually have low self esteem. Historically they started gambling at an early age, often in their teens, by placing small bets on sporting events or playing cards with friends or relatives. They progress through the four phases of the disorder over a 10- to 30-year time span.*
>
> *Action compulsive gamblers gamble primarily at 'skill' games such as poker or other card games; craps or other dice games; horse and dog racing and sports betting. Both legal and illegal sports betting is dominated by these gamblers. They gamble to beat other individuals or the House and often believe they can develop a system to achieve this goal. During the desperation phase of the disease, action gamblers often begin to gamble for escape, medicating the pain they are feeling from the destruction created by their gambling with the narcotic-like effect of slot or, more likely, video poker machines.*

'Escape' gamblers share some of these personality traits but with important differences. The authors refer to them as female because 94 per cent of women who called the ACCG telephone help line in 1999 were in this category. Of the men calling, 49 per cent were 'escapists'. Classic symptoms read as follows:

- Gambling becomes a problem later in life, frequently after 30 and as late as 80.
- Luck games are preferred – slot machines, video poker, bingo and the lottery.

- Players are numb, almost in a hypnotic-like state while gambling.
- They gamble to escape problems.
- They are free from physical and/or emotional pain while gambling.
- They are nurturing, responsible people for most of their adult lives.
- They are often victims of abuse.
- Confrontation is disliked. Empowerment is needed.
- Escapists have a harder time in early recovery because they have deep shame/ guilt feelings.
- They have a better chance of long-term recovery.

Hulen and Burns say an escape gambler quickly becomes enthralled by the slot, video poker and keno machine; 'it is exciting, it is fun, it does not talk back, it requires her full concentration...she realizes she has found a way to completely forget about all problems in her life. She feels comfortable, happy and free from turmoil. She may later report that, in retrospect, she realizes she was hooked the very first time she played.'

The escape gambler may been accompanied by family and friends during her first visits to the casino or arcade. But soon she's playing alone. No one tells her what to do, there are no demands or worries other than how to stay longer. Her social needs are met because the change girl and other gamblers know her face and start calling her by name. She makes friends with these regulars. She has also selected her favourite machine – 'her' machine – along with second and third favourites. The authors say:

> If she goes to the casino and someone else is at her machine she is angry. She will go to her second machine but would much rather be at her 'own' machine. She may talk to the machine telling it to 'come on, pay up', or swear at it and thank it when it pays, but she will usually go back to her machine time after time.
>
> A lady...accused her machine of infidelity when she saw another lady win a jackpot at it. However, as soon as the winner left she immediately returned to her machine, forgave its infidelity and continued the affair. Relationships with a machine are very real.

According to the Hulen-Burns paper, the four progressive phases of compulsive gambling apply equally to action-seekers and escapists. They are:

- The Winning Phase. This frequently lasts 3-5 years. Big wins - and especially big early wins - justify the gambler's belief that he's good, perhaps even 'professional'. He spends more and gambles more. Eventually, he begins to lose.

- The Losing Phase. Usually lasts more than five years. Gambling and losses continue to mount but the gambler is convinced it's just a losing streak. He bets on longshots, chases his losses, borrows betting money and begins to lie. He tries to show he's still a happy-go-lucky kinda guy and boasts about his wins, rarely mentioning his losses. This is strange because now he seems to lose all the time...

- The Desperation Phase. This can last for weeks or sometimes years. Now the gambler spends every waking hour either planning gambling or actively betting. He no longer controls his actions, lies frequently and is angry when lies are discovered. His family have either left or are on the verge of going. Debts are unmanageable and there may be criminal activity such as fraud or embezzlement. Incredibly, some gamblers will still keep up appearances and insist everything's under control. Action gamblers may by now have become escape gamblers. If they do try self-help recovery they will often blame others and fail to admit their own responsibilities. Some will stop long enough to win back their family...but it won't stop them betting again.

- The Hopeless Phase. Both action and escape gamblers have given up. They think no one can help them, that it matters little whether they live or die. Some will commit crimes knowing they face prison. Clinical depression is certain and all hopeless compulsives will consider suicide.

But do they ever pull the trigger? Come to that, does gambling ever lead to death by otherwise natural causes?

Not as far as US coroners are concerned. Between 1980 (the year pathological gambling became an 'official' disease in the US) and 1987 no death certificate has ever listed gambling as an underlying cause. There have been several attempts in the academic literature to challenge this mindset but with little success. As *The WAGER* said on 18 October 2000, 'The difficulties associated with determining necessary and sufficient causes and identifying partial causes has plagued this area of investigation.'

> A survey of 298 adult cocaine users found that 14.8 per cent of them had a lifetime history of compulsive gambling. The group was also more likely to have suffered severe psychiatric problems, alcoholism and attention deficit syndrome (ADD). Study by Steinberg et al: *Cocaine Abuse And Pathological Gambling*, 1992.

Take a 1990 study led by Donald R Jason, chief medical officer for Atlantic County, New Jersey, for example. He examined casino-related deaths between 1982 and 1986, beginning four years after the first legal casinos opened, and concluded: 'Our results indicate that gambling-related activities can be hazardous to one's health, especially among elderly cardiac patients.'

Jason's team found that of 398 casino-related deaths, 330 were sudden cardiac deaths of elderly white retired men. It decided that this figure was consistent with another study which showed that 'mortality...appeared to be greater among stricken gamblers than among others [non-casino] with similar cardiac attacks because surrounding patrons were preoccupied with their pursuit of profit and therefore failed to summon medical assistance.'

You can probably imagine the scene in the Casino Snuffit. 'Holy shit Ed, quit twitchin' an' turnin' blue an' pull yer fuckin' self together. Ain't no way I's foldin' a flush to call the medics.'

YOUNG, FREE AND GAMBLING

Despite the brisk business casinos provide for undertakers, many psychiatrists think occasional gambling may be good for older people. The importance of play in children is already well documented, and you don't need a degree to see why a trip to the racetrack could be fun for someone stuck at home.

We're still some way from doctors writing gambling prescriptions but in July 2002 the British Psychological Society discussed a paper from

Southampton University researcher Julie Winstone, which showed that older bingo players were better than elderly non-dabbers at number identification. 'Concentration has been shown to decline with age,' she said, 'bingo could be helping older people live longer' (quoted in *The Guardian*, 12 July 2002).

With schoolchildren you'd think the battle lines for pro- and anti-gambling campaigners would be clear. In some ways they are. A US meta-analysis – ie a study of studies – on 70+ research papers covering adolescents in the 13–20 age group (Shaffer and Hall, 1996) revealed that between 4.4 and 7.4 per cent of adolescents developed serious gambling problems. Between 9.9 and 14.2 per cent were classed as 'in transition'. These figures are far higher than those for similar studies on the general adult population.

Underage gambling is of course illegal almost everywhere but that's no problem if you wheel out your parents. A study of lottery ticket and scratchcard purchases in Britain ('The Acquisition, Development and Maintenance of Lottery and Scratchcard Gambling in Adolescence', *Journal Of Adolescence*, Wood and Griffiths, 1998) revealed that 57 per cent of 11-15 year olds reported that scratchcards had been bought for them by their mum or dad. With lottery tickets, this rose to 71 per cent. It's no exaggeration to say that if these figures are even remotely right they represent mass defiance of the law on a scale rarely seen in Britain.

At the North American Training Institute (NATI) director Elizabeth George believes a major public education programme is needed to warn parents of the risks. She told me:

Sometimes gambling is seen as a family affair. Very young children are taken to Las Vegas or the racetrack; grandparents who love these kids dearly buy them scratchcards for birthdays or Christmas stocking stuffers. Kids are the ultimate consumers and they get these positive messages about the excitement of gambling without any warning of the downside.

So far the data suggests adults don't see anything to warn about. In fact many believe they've finally found an activity for their kids that's fun, exciting and harmless so, hey, let's have a casino night at our school. Mom and dad dress up like Vegas blackjack dealers, they put out green felt to make craps tables, they hand out monopoly money and have a whip-round for prizes and reckon it'll be the best thing for the kids. And these are people who love children dearly. If you suggested a school cocktail night to introduce youngsters to alcohol they'd call you insane.

As a kid I remember going to the corner store to buy little packs of candy cigarettes. You'd hold them like a cigarette as you ate them. No one thought anything of it. Today it'd be like teaching your kids how to smoke. Gambling is fun. It's heavily promoted with exciting images of instant wealth, power, acceptance and freedom, and that makes it attractive.

George says American kids tend to start betting from an early age - on shooting baskets, playing pool - even tossing coins. A little older and they're organizing spread betting based on football or basketball national league results or running lottery syndicates. But card games are still number one.

They're ingrained in our culture. If the hockey team is travelling across town to play another school then the minute the bus pulls out the parking lot there's a poker game under way on the back seat. Mom and Dad are out of town for the weekend so Jimmy has 15 friends round to play poker. His parents think it's OK. Just a card game - that's surely fine.

We did one school survey to establish how many kids gambled. They told us they played poker every day. There was always a game at the table behind the post in the lunch hour. The school librarian didn't care as long as they were quiet. This goes back to the need to educate adults as much as children.

NATI's research reveals no single, obvious cause for addictive gambling in children. But the strong suggestion is that, for many, it has little to do with money. They gamble for the same reasons they might do drink or drugs. Problems at home, low self-esteem, the role-modelling of adults around them, avoiding pain or grief – in fact all the usual suspects.

> *If you have a youngster with a really unstable family life – violent or abusive parents, parents with alcohol and drug problems – then gambling becomes an escape from treacherous times at home.*
>
> *People love winners. Say you've got a 12-year-old kid with low self-esteem. He or she – and it's probably he because 70 per cent of child gamblers are boys – starts hanging out at an after-school poker game. Three nights in a row he walks out winning. Other kids look up to him. 'How'd you learn to play poker so well?' 'Here, touch me, let's have some of that luck rub off.' This is heady stuff for an insecure kid.*
>
> *Winning is a powerful hook. If our 12-year-old has picked up $75, he'll feel on top of the world; he has a temporary respite from the inferiority he feels. In his position, wouldn't you play again?*

For students with a manageable habit the reasons for gambling are diverse. Social life is certainly one factor, but in a study of US psychology students (Lostustter *et al*, 2002) only 11 per cent gave this as their prime motivation. Money (42 per cent) and fun (23 per cent) both came out higher with excitement a poor fourth (7.3 per cent). The other scoring categories – winning, competition, risk-taking and boredom – managed only 16.1 per cent between them. As more research is published it's becoming clear that there are very few 'givens' so far as young gamblers are concerned.

Dr Howard Shaffer, director of the Division on Addictions at Harvard Medical School, offers a good example of the way American public assumptions are being challenged. 'It is stunning,' he says, 'that in Nevada, the state with by far the most gambling outlets, the rate of youthful gambling is the lowest in the country. People have actually avoided discussing this because they fear it would lead to deregulation of gambling in other places.

'Sometimes when you let the genie out of the bottle it's hard to get it back in. I understand those concerns. And yet a good public health model would encourage rigorous evaluation to see if we can figure out why the Nevada effect has happened and learn from it.'

An investigation into the illegal sale of keno tickets to minors in Massachusetts (Harshbarger, 1996) discovered that children made successful purchases 66 per cent of the time. Fewer than half the sales agents displayed legal notices about minimum age requirements.

NURTURE OR NATURE

The age-old 'nurture-or-nature' cliché, which surfaces in most arguments about human behaviour, is never knowingly under-used where gambling is concerned. But it is interesting to speculate on how access to money, type of job and lifestyle *may* be a factor in the speed with which a problem gambler heads down the slippery slope. A study of 3,852 workers at an unidentified US gaming corporation discovered that 2.1 per cent were level-three compulsive gamblers (twice the rate in the general population) and 9.8 per cent had MDEs or 'major depressive episodes' (3.7 per cent generally) (from 'Gambling, Drinking, Smoking and other Health Risk Activities Among Casino Employees', *American Journal of Industrial Medicine*, Shaffer, Vander Bilt & Hall, 1999). Yet for level-two problem gamblers, the casino figure was a third lower than for the general population – 1.4 per cent as opposed to 2.2.

This 1999 study by Shaffer *et al* tries to explain the contradiction by noting how casino employees witness problem gambling first hand. Understanding the dangers may serve as a protective factor against development of sub-clinical level-two problem gambling but is still not strong enough to prevent some people slipping all the way to level three.

The same is true of problem gamblers with access to large amounts of money at work. Not all will steal from their employers because they understand the risk of getting caught and the consequences. But some will take that extra step. Take these examples from the *Daily Telegraph*.

'Pensions Fiddled To Pay For Gambling' (26 September 1996). This article tells how a village sub-postmistress falsified £4,652 ($2,978) worth of pension claims to feed her addiction to National Lottery scratchcards.

'Another Six Months For Lottery Addict' (8 January 1999): This is a court report on a Samaritans branch manager who stole £36,000 ($54,000) from the charity to satisfy a 'compulsive addiction' to scratchcards. She fraudulently obtained an additional £7,700 ($11,550) from a bank while she was on bail awaiting sentence.

'Bank Chief Fights Sack Over Gambling' (November 8, 2000): This story concerned a bank manager who ran up debts of almost £80,000 ($120,000) through fruit-machine gambling. He appealed against the bank's decision to sack him. The bank claimed that he'd lied about loans.

FOOTBALLERS' PREDISPOSITION...

For problem gamblers newspaper headlines hardly represent the best careers advice. But if you've a betting weakness *and* a gifted right foot you should think hard before becoming a professional footballer. Fifty grand a week may seem a lot, but in the English Premiership you can blow that away in a card school on your way to the game. Pots of £7,000 ($10,050) are not uncommon and during Euro 2000 a group of stars reportedly had £10,000 ($15,000) riding on one hand.

There's a story in the football business about a manager who taps up a player he wants to sign. 'First son,' says the manager, 'I need to know your personal problem. Is it booze, drugs or women? Because I'll find out sooner or later.' Funny he didn't ask about gambling. The UK charity Sporting Chance estimates that 10 per cent of professional players are addicted. No club, it says, is totally clean.

'If you have the kind of driven, obsessive character that it takes to become a professional footballer, with that tunnel vision, then you are pre-disposed,' says Peter Kay, chief executive of the charity (quoted in the *Independent*, 16 January 2003). 'I have not come across a football club where gambling does not play a part in the players' lives.

'The problem is made worse because players have huge amounts of money to spend, lots of time on their hands and are, often, lonely especially as they travel a lot and spend long hours in hotels.' The charity's main backer, former England and Arsenal central defender Tony Adams, agrees. 'Alcohol was my addiction but gambling is rife in the game,' he says. 'At least, that is my observation.'

January 2003 saw open season on soccer gamblers. First up was Chelsea's Icelandic international striker Eidur Gudjohnsen who gave an in-depth interview to *The People* under the headline: 'I won £100k in just one night...then ended up losing nearly half a million. I knew if I didn't stop I'd lose everything.'

The People said the '24-year-old blond heart-throb' blamed a combination of boredom, loneliness and the buzz from a run of beginner's luck as the cause of his problems.

> *When I had that huge win I had a feeling of elation which I can only compare to the adrenaline rush of scoring a goal. It put me on a high and it was magical. But it was a false feeling. I was looking for a quick fix but it just made things worse then they were already.*
>
> *It got to the point where I was just chasing the money that I had won initially and was getting dragged deeper and deeper. I have seen for myself just how dangerous this gambling thing can be. I will definitely not put another foot in the casino. I can easily see how young people can get sucked into gambling and I am happy to stand up as a warning to others not to get hooked.*

The following week it was England star Michael Owen's turn. The *Sunday Mirror* claimed he had spent £2 million ($3 million) on horseracing and spread betting, including a loss of £26,000 ($39,000) in a single day. The previous year Owen had been fingered by various sports writers as the player who lost £30,000 ($45,000) in an England players' card school during the 2002 World Cup. He has denied this and insisted his gambling is 'nowhere near' the amounts claimed.

That same Sunday the *News Of The World* published an investigation under the headline: 'Every one a loser. The names...the dates...the money...the dossier that will shame football.' The story catalogued the betting habits of four leading Premiership stars who, according to the *NOW*, had together wagered £1,285,435 ($1,928,153) in visits to London's Grosvenor Casinos.

The *Sunday Mirror* piece also quoted Dr Austin Tate, medical director of the UK's Priory rehabilitation centre and a consultant psychiatrist to the Football Association. 'Footballers competing at the highest level have admitted that they can't get off the pitch quick enough to see who's won the 4.45 at Haydock,' he said.

'[Footballers]...have the money and more importantly have the time. If they get addicted then they will wake up thinking about it and go to sleep thinking about it. It gets to a stage where they don't care about money. All they want is the buzz of winning...a footballer who takes to the field with a gambling habit will not find it possible to concentrate on the game properly. He'll just be thinking about the horses or the dogs or the cards.'

On 4 May 2003 the *Mail On Sunday* published perhaps the most illuminating interview yet on the demons faced by soccer's gamblers. In it the 35-year-old former England and Arsenal player Paul Merson told how he'd once turned over £80,000 ($120,000) in a single day's betting and lost £30,000 ($45,000) backing Holland to beat Ireland in a World Cup qualifier.

'I've stayed away from drink and drugs,' said Merson, whose cocaine and alcohol problems have been well documented, 'but gambling has beat me, spanked me all over the place. This is one of the biggest killers in the world. Every day it would go through my head about committing suicide.' He goes on:

People talk about getting alcoholic blackouts, well, I get gambling blackouts. The war with Iraq had been going on for a week before I noticed. I live in my own secret world where I bet on anything.

I am a complete and utter compulsive gambler. I have sat in a hotel room and contemplated smashing my fingers just so I wouldn't be able to pick up the telephone to ring my bookmaker. I have been on so many holidays with the kids to Florida yet I have never been on a single ride at Disney World. How sad is that? All I want to do is have my next bet. I just gambled every day, on the Internet or on the phone. If I lose £10,000, instead of thinking I have to get it back over the next month I have to get it back in the next 10 minutes.

When I'm gambling, I don't want to be around anybody. I don't talk to anybody. I just go into another world. Then I lie in bed and think the phone bill is due or the bank statement is coming so I get up to meet the postman and get the letters before my wife sees them.

This is compulsive gambling at its most scary and sinister. Deceit rules. Lies tumble out effortlessly. Loved ones are kicked mercilessly aside. And you don't need to be dripping with money either.

Just ask Andy...

AN ADDICT'S STORY
In researching this book I spoke to perhaps half a dozen gamblers in various stages of recovery or addiction. The idea was to tell their individual stories but after interviewing them there wasn't much point. Give or take the odd anecdote, it was all pretty much the same.

So Andy became my pen portrait of a typical problem gambler. Now aged 38 he lives with his partner in a modest, detached house in the west of England. When they moved in six years ago they were mortgage-free. Now they have a mortgage of £115,000 ($172,500). As you've probably already guessed, Andy hasn't quite managed to stop gambling.

But then, as he'll tell you, it's in his blood. As a kid growing up on the edge of London he remembers the excitement he felt feeding fruit machines and, occasionally, pocketing the winnings. His dad owned and trained greyhounds so it was natural to travel around meetings. Sometimes they would do three a day. Always, they'd have a bet.

By the time he left school Andy was into horseracing. He'd bet between £200 ($300) and £300 ($450) per week, sometimes losing £160 ($240) in an afternoon. It didn't worry him though. 'I could afford to lose,' he said. 'I was a single guy and there were plenty of jobs. I had plenty of money.' But while working in a betting office during the mid-1980s he found the losses mounting. One week he was short on the mortgage money and says he asked permission from his boss to borrow petty cash. The following day head office staged a surprise audit and both men were sacked. Andy was prosecuted and got 200 hours' community service.

By 1991 his gambling addiction had bitten. Big wins on the Derby (from stakes placed on his wedding day) and at Royal Ascot saw him pick up £1,000 ($1,500) in winnings over a few weeks. It vanished just as quickly. Now working for a bookie in Aylesbury he begun dipping his hands in the safe. Another audit, another few hundred quid short, another court appearance, another 200 hours. And no job.

Britain's gambling industry is facing an 'addict tax' to fund therapy for betting addicts. In 2003 the UK government hinted that it would impose a compulsory levy unless big business contributed £3 million ($4.5 million) per year.

With his wife at work, he was now home alone and bored. 'I was desperate to bet,' he recalls, 'so, obviously, I started selling household items. I got rid of the fridge, the cooker, the hoover, the telly and every time I found some kind of excuse. Usually I blamed the bailiffs. But when I sold our car my wife upped and left. I think the few hundred quid I got lasted a couple of days down the bookie.'

Weeks later – now living with an aunt – he attended his first Gamblers Anonymous session. For a while he stayed clear of betting shops and his aunt's watchful eye ensured he kept up the therapy. But after 18 months he moved out. Secretly he still craved the gambling buzz and soon he was back in the old routine. 'I'd gamble for two or three hours,' he said, 'and it felt like total freedom. Afterwards I'd walk away thinking, God what have you done. I knew it was wrong but I couldn't stop. I spent every last penny.'

Inevitably Andy was evicted and began sleeping rough in a caravan he found rusting in a builders' yard. Like so many gamblers he was good at hiding his demons and eventually he got night shifts at a 24-hour motorway service station, slogging through 60- and 70-hour weeks. It allowed him the luxury of a few hours' sleep on the staff-room couch and a breath of normality. In December 1997 he fell for Sandra, another employee. Incredibly, six years later she's still with him.

Incredibly? Well, would you stick with a partner who'd borrowed your cash card and sneakily wiped out £5,000 ($7,500)? A partner who denied responsibility every time and blamed the bank? Who blew £4,000 ($6,000) in weeks during a bender on fruit machines? Who forced you to take out a new mortgage to settle his debts – then pawned the gold bracelet you got for your 21st birthday for 90 quid's betting money? Andy did all these things even though he clearly loves Sandra and has nightmares about hurting her. 'I knew I'd be in the shit every time,' he said. 'And I was a shit. But I could no more stop gambling than I could stop breathing.'

Sandra finds it hard to explain her patience. As if there aren't enough issues in her life she suffers from a crippling form of arthritis. Sometimes, on bad days, Andy has to carry her around the house. 'There are times when I've wanted to punch and punch him until I could punch no more,' she says. 'But I don't know many men who would stick by me and nurse me like he has. He's a diamond but he has this addiction that's so much stronger than him.'

She knows he is still gambling. He claims he has it under control; that he can walk away whether he's winning or losing. He insists the deceit has ended.

Time will tell with Andy...

HEALTHY FUTURES

The rueful joke among general practitioners is that healthcare doesn't make a lot of difference. No matter what you do, in a large enough random sample of patients a third will get better, a third will get worse and the rest will stay the same. It's a bit like that with gambling cures. It's not that they don't work; it's that they *all* work but not always impressively. At Harvard this has demanded some hard thinking from Howard Shaffer and his colleagues.

> There are very few treatment outcome studies. Those that have been done have primarily focused on cognitive behavioural treatments and what we know is that those treatments work. We also know that for some reason they aren't attractive to people with addictions, in fact they seem to repel some people. This is not

to say we can't make them more attractive or that we won't find other effective methods. The problem is that without more outcome studies we can't identify things that really are beneficial.

Cognitive treatment pays most attention to the way people think about what they're doing, rather than any physiological or genetic aspect. In other words, how they plan their behaviour and the internal dialogue which determines what they actually do. A cognitive approach tries to change the addictive behaviour.

For example, one of the most effective treatments teaches people about the independence of random events and that when you gamble you have no control. Even the smartest gamblers tend to think that after ten straight losses the chances of winning might be greater, when in fact they are the same.

He dislikes labels such as 'problem' and 'pathological', preferring instead the levels system (see above). This defines the degree of a gambler's compulsion in a similar way to burns (ie first or second degree), stages of cancer and types of diabetes. It's a method widely adopted by public health administrators as a way of allocating resources. Shaffer says:

Personally I find the term pathological offensive. It doesn't encourage anyone to participate in the treatment system, rather it implicitly repels people and stigmatizes them in a way that reflects an old-fashioned viewpoint on addiction. It encourages the idea that addiction is a personal attribute that's not very changeable, whereas in fact evidence suggests that people with addictive behaviours change much more often than scientists and lay people alike think.

Human beings are still on earth because, unlike the dinosaurs, we're far more adaptive than any of our social critics give credit for. If you look at history, every new technology, every opportunity to take risks was going to be the downfall of the human race. At each turn we've adapted. Sometimes it took longer; sometimes it came quicker and sometimes at considerable social cost. I'm not *trying to say these changes are always benign. But people do react to potentially unhealthy situations. And they do change their behaviour.*

What we can say is that no matter what people experience in treatment, on balance they improve. We've found that with other addictive behaviours as well. This gets to a very interesting and progressive way of thinking about gambling and other addictions. Maybe they're not so different. Maybe they have an underlying similarity so that no matter what you do it'll work on some aspect of the addiction.

It's so easy to say that a treatment does or doesn't work when in fact we can only make statements about the areas that have been studied. Very, very little treatment work in gambling has been studied.

This is one reason why Shaffer would like to see much greater emphasis on gambling addiction as a public health issue. When he and a colleague, David Korn, first floated this notion they expected a backlash from scientists, politicians and lobbyists. Instead they found a refreshing willingness to listen.

We have been very surprised at the rapid embracement of the idea. Having said that, people hear the words 'public health perspective' and they think we're gathering ammunition to be anti-gambling. In fact a public health perspective requires us to be balanced and to look at different viewpoints. While our suggestions have been embraced, they still aren't widely understood. That phase is just beginning.

People perceive gambling as a public health issue largely because it's in our environment; it's everywhere we look. It has the same properties – the same feel –as other potential environmental pollutants. Almost as though it's a germ you can catch.

In the past we've suggested gambling problems are the result of individual attributes. Now we're saying it's probably more complicated than that. It's part of our culture, part of our environment. It's woven into the fabric of our experience – it isn't just a personality or psychological state.

People forget that psychiatric and diagnostic criteria are simply the codification of public opinion and public opinion is shaped by culture and experience. Intemperate gambling has been around for centuries but in that time the view of what is intemperate has shifted. My colleague Bob Bernhart at the University of Las Vegas quite rightly points out that the group that punished gambling most in American history was the religious right. Now, curiously, the religious right is coming to its aid by arguing for more regulations and restrictions, as if that will protect people. Actually, it might make things worse.

Governments are in a complicated position here. In many ways they have a conflict of interest. We could relieve their conflict if governments simply licensed private organizations to be purveyors of gambling, taxed them accordingly and used the tax dollars to protect the public.

In my opinion, governments should not be in the gambling business at all. But they are and as a result of this, and having a stake in the treatment side and the distribution of resources, they are serving many masters. Unfortunately gambling disorders, like many others, have low prevalence rates and that makes it easy for politicians to blame the victims.

Shaffer hopes Britain will use gambling deregulation as a chance to declare stated public policies for tackling addiction – policies that can be properly monitored and evaluated for short- and long-term changes. 'Unfortunately,' he sighs, 'most governments do not do that. In Nevada, the most gambling-intensive part of the US, there is some evidence to suggest that over many years people have come to a balance with the gambling opportunities there. While at another point in history this did not appear so. We have to build in to public policy a way of watching what the policy does rather than simply assuming that politicians know best.'

THE NEUROBIOLOGY OF GAMBLING ADDICTION

I know, I know. Neurobiology is one of those scary, turn-the-page type of words. But so far as addiction is concerned what we're really talking about here is the science of pleasure. Why cold beer on hot days? Why isn't dishwashing better than sex? How come people love chocolate ahead of mashed turnip? And what is it about hugging your kids that makes you *feel* love?

There are lots of evolutionary theories as to why our brains approve of certain everyday actions. Cold beer soothes an over-heating body. Sex – the biggest natural high – is crucial to the survival of the species. Chocolate is a rich energy source. The buzz you get from hugging your kids ensures you nurture them to become adults – well, hopefully.

When we feel these pleasures the brain sends out a chemical messenger as a reward – 'you did good, do that again' is how one US psychiatrist once put it to me. These chemicals, or neurotransmitters, help govern every mental and physical function we perform and the process is all but instantaneous.

Having a pleasurable moment therefore works like this. The brain analyzes something it likes and sends an electrical impulse down cells known as neurons. The last of these, called a *pre*-synaptic cell, is prodded into releasing a chemical neurotransmitter such as serotonin or dopamine into a gap between the neurons known as the synapse.

The neurotransmitter triggers an electrical impulse in a neighbouring *post*-synaptic cell and, hey presto, does that feel cool or what? Transporters mooching about in the synapse then round up and return the pleasure chemicals to their pre-synaptic cell ready for next time. That's called re-uptake.

There are many ways in which this process can be disrupted but recent research has focused heavily on the re-uptake transporters. If they re-absorb too much then they effectively suck all the ordinary, everyday tootling along kind of pleasure out of your synapses – leading to depression. Common drugs called selective serotonin re-uptake inhibitors (SSRIs) have been developed to combat this. Prozac, Zoloft, Paxil, Celexa and Luvox are among the best known.

Pleasure transmitters such as dopamine and serotonin are being released into the synapses all the time but they can't just be left there making us constantly happy. If they did, how would we distinguish between evolutionarily useful and wasteful experiences? This is why re-uptake transporters play such a crucial role, a role also key to the effects of recreational drugs.

Psychiatrists know that drugs like cocaine disrupt re-uptake by attaching themselves to dopamine transporters and disabling them. Having all that dopamine swilling around the synapses creates the typical 30- or 40-minute coke rush. Once it's over, the brain gets very tetchy and starts rounding up so many dopamine messengers that levels fall well below normal. This is what a user colloquially terms the 'crash'. So how do users deal with this depressing, despairing feeling? They snort more coke. Here lies the essence of addiction.

The more we get to know about the brain's chemical processes the better our chances of understanding problem gambling. Knowledge of dopamine is high on the Most Wanted list because scientists are already fairly sure it is implicated. A study by Swedish researchers has shown that it is deficient in the brains of compulsive gamblers, although it's not clear whether the gambling causes this, whether the lower dopamine level causes the gambling or whether both are associated with other factors.

One of those factors might lie in our DNA, the 'gambling genes' that make some of us particularly vulnerable. The mapping of the human genome is expected to produce major advances in this area and much interest has already focused on the 5-HTT gene, which governs the performance of serotonin re-uptake transporters. It is among 27 million bases within human chromosome 17. Another promising candidate is the D-2 gene, known to be stimulated in some people by drugs, sex, food and gambling.

Intriguingly, nerve impulses triggered by gambling cause changes both in blood flow and electrical activity within the brain. One study (Rogers, Owen, Middleton, Williams, Pickard, Sahakian and Robbins, 1999) recorded these changes in the middle frontal gyrus, inferior frontal gyrus and orbital gyrus of the brain. More meaningfully for gamblers, it seems there is also a 'little devil' crackle of electrical activity that encourages them to be reckless when luck isn't going their way. According to a study by Dr William Gehring of the University of Michigan, this process is linked to an area between the brain's two hemispheres, the anterior cingulate cortex. 'It's the gambler's fallacy: if you lose money you think you are due for a win,' said Dr Gehring. 'Here's a brain system that's tuned the same way' (quoted in the *Daily Telegraph* 22 March 2003).

'As a result when we make a quick decision and it turns out to be wrong we tend to take a bigger risk the next time than we would have done if our first choice had been right. We can evaluate the outcomes of these decisions before we've even consciously thought about what we're doing.'

The drug Naltrexone, developed in 1994 to treat heroin addiction and alcoholism, has been shown to reduce the urges facing compulsive gamblers according to a series of recent American studies.

Doesn't seem like evolution has served us well on this one. 'Our brains are probably tuned to be poor in situations where things happen by chance,' added Dr Gehring. 'In the real world there are usually many cases where a string of bad will usually be followed by something good. At some point several days of rain will stop and be followed by sun.' Not if you live in Manchester. Still, he makes his point.

What does all this mean for treatment? The SSRI drugs may well treat addiction symptoms but there's little sign that they tackle underlying causes. Pills designed to control the gambling urge are being trialled but are light years from achieving 'magic bullet' status. Aversion therapy, in which compulsive gamblers are wired up and given electric shocks as they look at images of casinos or horseracing, was abandoned in the 1970s as cruel, unethical and mostly unsuccessful. The same fate met 'saturation' therapy where racing punters were forced to bet on an endless series of taped races with a nurse acting as runner.

Today most treatment involves self-help or cognitive behaviour therapy (see above) based on counselling or 12-step programmes. The British gambling charity Gamcare has reported a 46 per cent success rate with its group counselling sessions (*BBC News Online*, 26 January 2001). Success was measured according to whether the gambler still experienced problems six months later. The 12 steps, beginning with 'I admit that I am powerless over my addiction', encourage compulsive gamblers to throw themselves at the mercy of God as they 'understand him'. The programme also focuses on making amends for actions and accepting personal responsibility.

One of the greatest difficulties facing healthcare providers is that they can't predict who's most at risk. Without an ability to predict, says Howard Shaffer, we can't claim to have an explanation for addiction:

> *The conventional wisdom is that things like drugs or gambling cause addiction. Whereas I think addiction is much more the result of the relationship between a person and a thing. The thing itself is not the cause. I'm afraid this makes the issue more complicated but then that's what academics do. We complicate things.*
>
> *At the University of Virginia, Dr Kenneth Kendler has reported an excellent study (American Journal of Psychiatry, May 2003) showing that our genetic predispositions are not specific to certain types of addiction, they're more generic. Which addiction you might develop is a function of your experience.*
>
> *We certainly have new evidence that the brain processes involved with drug addiction are also involved with gambling. The problem is that the research is not precise. What we know is that there are shifts in neurochemistry when people anticipate gambling, while they gamble and probably as a consequence of gambling – just as there is with the appreciation of female beauty by men and the anticipation of drug use or with drug use.*
>
> *In the case of drugs you have imposter chemical molecules; with gambling or beauty you have the shifting of natural chemical molecules. The problem is that we don't know what these shifts mean – whether they're limited to things that encourage continued use or to help us, for example, distinguish outcomes in our environment.*
>
> *Our brain is always making bets about what will happen. When what we expect will happen happens, we get a different neuro-*

chemical shift to that when we are surprised. It's hard to know whether these shifts are actually trouble, in an addiction sense, or whether they are simply monitoring tools to help us understand the world around us.

Makes you wonder doesn't it? If we ever do nail down the neurobiology of gambling we can perhaps start to understand other complex, highly driven emotional experiences such as love and hate, winning and losing.

And, of course, cheating...

MONEY

> 'Trust everybody. But cut the cards.'
>
> – Finley Peter Dunne, *Mr Dooley's Philosophy*

When this book was conceived, a chapter on the economics of gambling seemed like a good plan. You know the sort of thing: political lobbying, investment returns, social cost-benefit analysis, the impact of new laws, Internet gaming etc. But as most of this stuff has already squirrelled its way onto previous pages this chapter is now mostly devoted to those who make their mark – sometimes literally – in the darker side of gambling. Who are they? Dirty rotten cheats and scoundrels, that's who!

Now it's quite wrong that criminals should benefit from ripping off immensely rich, exclusive casinos or profit out of some honest bookmaker or make millions out of an inept management that has put too much faith in software security. Of course it's wrong and yet...it's hard to suppress the feeling that it serves the bastards right. Perhaps it's down to that old adage about living and dying by the sword. Anyway, with apologies to the gambling industry for the merest hint of *schadenfreude*, here goes.

First, how to define gambling crime. According to the American Gaming Association (AGA) it's all a put-up job as far as casinos are concerned. 'Anecdotal information and popular myth have perpetuated claims by gambling opponents that casinos are linked to increased crime rates in communities and organized crime,' says AGA's 2003 Crime Fact Sheet. 'However, nearly all recent publicly and privately funded studies, as well as the testimony of law enforcement agents from around the country, refute these claims.

It goes on to quote from a tidal wave of helpful research and makes the point that 'those who attribute an increase in crime to the presence of casinos routinely fail to account for the fact that casinos are significant tourist destinations. When this influx of people is properly accounted for, there is no increase in crime rates when comparing pre and post-casino periods.'

For the moment we'll leave aside the sea of dirty money swilling around Monaco's casinos and accept that, in the US at least, the industry has all but shed its Mafia-money tag and general sleazebag image. Casino profits depend on licences, and managers need to be incredibly stupid to risk alienating cops and local politicians by running disorderly operations. But in the gambling business generally, a narrow definition of crime as something one person does to another at a specific place just won't do.

If I've bribed a footballer, jockey, cricketer or basketball player to fix a major sporting event, and placed stakes online or via telephone in London, Las Vegas, Sydney, Hong Kong and Johannesburg, where has the crime happened? 'Nothing to do with us', the bookies will cry. 'How could we know? We're victims too y'know.' Except that they sold the faulty goods – ie the bet – didn't they? Suppose you run a grocery shop that poisons its customers with dodgy pre-packed prawns. Try telling the UK trading standards people it's nothing to do with you!

The point is that gambling crime is a multi-headed, multi-national monster. It encompasses tax evasion (big winnings are taxable in the US), under-age betting, unlicensed bookies, cheating at cards or roulette, fixing sports events, illegal advertising, credit card thieves (who like drawing cash advances at casinos on stolen cards), slot machine fraudsters, money launderers, protection racketeers, loan sharks...the list goes on. All legal businesses making money from gambling have a duty to help tackle these crimes. And all honest gamblers should mind very much if they don't.

MAKING LINKS
It's not that easy to draw a line between gambling and non-gambling offences. At the Alberta Gaming Research Institute in Canada Professor Garry Smith, one of the world's leading authorities on gambling-related

crime, is trying to harden up data by reviewing classifications in police files. It's proving a long haul. He says:

> We've interviewed police officers, gambling security personnel, government officials – essentially any organization which might improve the picture. We've also carried out crime-mapping, where we input the location of a major gaming venue and see the amount and type of crimes that occur over a year.
>
> The big problem is that, very often, police don't list a motive or say what stolen money has been used for. Has a man battered his wife because he happened to get drunk and violent? Or has he lost money at the casino and is taking it out on her? Similarly, we could be looking at crimes perpetuated by problem gamblers to support their addiction; breach-of-trust offences like forgery, embezzlement and fraud. But if the file doesn't mention it, we'll never know. Gambling has lost its stigma and it's hard for the police to get enthused about tackling it – even though there's the potential for an organized crime element.
>
> We're finding a significant amount of gambling-related crime and illegal gambling. Direct offences, such as cheating at play, or indirect in the sense that a venue attracts criminal types because of the money that's involved and the opportunity to launder. This is not an attack on casinos; banks and shopping centres attract criminals in precisely the same way.

Smith says Ontario's provincial police force has established a clear link between gambling and organized crime. It's more overt on Canada's east coast (because of the closer geographical links to gambling in America's eastern cities) and key players tend to be Asian crime groups, motorcycle gangs and ethnic criminals dealing with their own nationalities in enclaves. From Smith again:

> Mostly, these people are running illegal books. Some commentators claim it's a victimless crime, given that the same thing happens

legally. The difficulty with that argument is that underworld gambling runs alongside loan-sharking – giving credit for bets and then beating up anyone who can't pay on time. It's also clear that money garnered from illegal games goes on to finance other illegal activities such as drug pushing.

I'm afraid governments will always try to side-step the issue. Ten years ago they were denying that problem gambling even existed. Now they say there's just a small percentage of victims and that money is going into treatment and research programmes. The truth is that most governments remain blind to gambling's risks because of the revenue it brings them.

My concern is that if it's all made legal there will be more outlets for people who gamble. The small percentage susceptible to an addiction will get more exposure and there's a greater chance that more will commit crimes to support their habit.

CHEATING THE CASINO

To a non-gambler there's something vaguely baffling about professional casinos being cheated by card and roulette players. Surely this sort of thing belongs in Victorian fairgrounds and Wild West saloons? How can cheats prosper when there are enough gaming floor cameras to service a Jennifer Lopez photo-call? As for those large Men In Black security types, what do they actually *do*?

The truth is that casino games are still low-tech. That's what makes them fun. Virtual reality is fine but there's nothing like picking up your cards or wanging down your chips for that hands-on feel-good factor. And wherever you've got fast hands and human watchdogs you've got the chance to cheat.

In Britain, Inspector Ben Bhangoo of London's Metropolitan Police has a unique view of this daily battleground. As officer-in-charge of the Gaming Unit he goes after cheats of any and all makes: organized gangs, bent dealers, team players and the gifted single-handed scamster. There's always someone prepared to have a go, whatever the risk and in spite of casino defences. It's never easy money. But it's often BIG money.

Like most senior policemen Bhangoo wants more staff to engage the enemy. He's also realistic enough to know it isn't going to happen. 'The Gaming Unit must be the smallest department in the Met,' he told me. 'At the moment it's just me and a manager who runs the office.

'If you spoke to the Commissioner he'd say gaming isn't a policing priority; it's burglaries and street crime and all the rest. I'd kind of agree with that but you can't just ignore gambling totally. Our unit has years of experience and it takes many man-hours to investigate gaming crime. If we take on that burden it allows the local police station to tackle the Commissioner's priorities.'

A career police officer, Bhangoo was born in Kenya, East Africa, and emigrated to Britain in the 1960s. He joined the Met as a 19-year-old PC in 1973 and served at various London police stations, the Police Training College and the TSG (Territorial Support Group) riot squad. He's been around the block a few times and so when he joined the Gaming Unit in 1999 he fully expected to encounter conmen, villains and Mafia types. He said:

I shared a common misconception, which dates from pre-1968. It is that casinos make money through rogue roulette wheels and dodgy dealers. In fact the industry is very well managed and regulated. Casino bosses would never risk losing their licence because it's worth so much to them.

Before 1968 there were serious problems in the UK gaming industry. We had over 100 casinos in central London and there were plenty of criminals involved because it was such easy money. Drinking, gambling and prostitution all went hand in hand. Then the government brought in the 1968 Gaming Act and set up the Gaming Board for Great Britain, which still does an excellent job today.

The Gaming Board did its background checks and the criminals were cleared out. The number of casinos was drastically reduced and now we have 24 in London, which is still more than any other capital city. Of these, we define seven as upper market, eleven as mid-market and five at the lower end. These are broad categories based on turnover.

At the lower end more people go in but they don't gamble such large amounts. Up at the top a few will lose millions to keep the owners happy. Some casinos will have a minimum 50p bet; others are reluctant to take less than a fiver. You also find minimum stakes tend to be raised as the night wears on and it gets busier.

Gaming Board rules demand that all casino staff have a certificate if they're handling money. These are graded according to levels of responsibility – red for head cashiers and pit bosses, green for inspectors and supervisors, grey for managers and white for executives. Their names go to the UK's Criminal Records Bureau and they are asked to declare previous convictions. Bhangoo says that declaring a record isn't necessarily a bar: 'In fact, it shows people are dealing with their past honestly.'

None of the dealers, security staff, pit bosses, general managers and casino executives are allowed to take tips. Waitresses or reception staff are permitted because they can't influence a game. As for the tables themselves, every one is covered by security cameras, along with reception areas and the cashier's office.

Something like 90 per cent of casino crime is carried out by guest players. There's no way of immediately verifying their details so they use false names and addresses and get signed in by a crooked casino member. 'When I start investigating,' says Bhangoo 'my first question to the member is, "Who's your guest?" He'll insist he met the guy in a café outside. Never seen him before but signed him in because he fancied a go at gambling. You can't prosecute that member without proof of collusion. And it's very difficult to trace the guest. Some individuals have used 15 false names and addresses in this way.'

Criminal gangs occasionally target the casinos and in the spring of 2003 five of Bhangoo's nine investigations involved Turks. One prosecution came to court in May when Reset Ertas, 45, and Mesut Yil, 33, both from Istanbul, pleaded guilty to cheating the Ritz Hotel casino at poker. They were caught on camera swapping cards under the table and were arrested as they tried to cash £4,800 ($7,200) worth of chips. A further £8,000 ($12,000) they'd won earlier in the evening was never recovered. Both men got six months.

Ertas and Yil were working on their own account but, according to senior Scotland Yard detectives, gambling, prostitution, firearms, drugs and refugee smuggling have all become major markets for the ethnic criminal underworld. In October 2002 police recovered an AK47 assault rifle plus large quantities of ammunition during an investigation into turf wars between rival Turkish gangs. They know it could just as easily have been Albanians, Asians, Southeast Asians, Chinese or Jamaicans – most of whom compete within their own ethnic groups. 'Once those power struggles are won or lost,' said the Yard's Deputy Assistant Commissioner Mike Fuller, 'we believe there is the potential for ethnic inter-gang conflict. We are determined to stop that happening.'

A SPOTTER'S GUIDE TO ROULETTE CHEATS

Roulette, Ben Bhangoo tells me, is the casino cheat's sting-of-choice. To understand why, we need to see how the game is organized and operated. First, you have to know your chips. Each table has a range of different colours bearing the same motif. Perhaps you'll ask a dealer for your yellow chips to be worth £2 ($3) each. You can only use them at his table; they won't be accepted at others where yellows carry greater value. At any one table, everyone picks a colour and sticks to it.

You can also play with cash chips. This is a straightforward exchange – the chips are marked with the amount they're worth – and generally only one player per table plays with them to avoid confusion and disputes.

Above you cameras run constantly, although not for the convenience of the police. 'Don't I know it,' Bhangoo told me. 'The cameras are based so that you can see the dealer, the roulette table and the wheel. The main aim is to stop dealers cheating the casino.'

Disputes tend to centre on the ownership of a winning cash chip or the placing of chips. Dealers will often 'tidy up' a table before spinning the wheel but they don't always check if a bet is in the intended square. Roulette gamblers may argue that they backed a winning number when they actually covered a dividing line (a split bet, paid at lower odds of 17-1). Such problems invariably demand a replay of the tapes.

Detecting a roulette cheat is difficult enough at the best of times but if you fancy a go (at detecting that is, not cheating) here's the *This Is Gambling* handy 'spotter's guide':

THE SLEIGHT-OF-HAND MERCHANT

Often this thief will wait for a busy layout with a lot of cash chips. He'll scoop up these chips in the same hand movement used to place his own. Mostly it's just sleight of hand, although some players fix sticky tape to their palms to make it easier (also known as check copping). Often a big cash player won't even realize he's a victim. He may have thrown his chips on without caring which numbers he's backed.

THE DOUBLE CHIPPER

Here a gambler has a high value-chip in the palm of her hand and another in her fingers. As the ball falls into place she drops the first chip from her palm onto the winning number and in the same motion bets on a different number with the chip in her fingers. The dealer sees only the second placement and returns it as a late bet. The winning chip stays in position.

THE COLUMN-PUSHER

This gambler stands at a column end (the roulette numbers are grouped into three columns) and you'll see his chips hand hovering as he waits for the ball to drop. Any column bet that comes up pays at 2-1. The pusher waits until the very last second and then eases his chip onto the right column. 'There are some very clever players out there who know the table layout inside out,' says Bhangoo. 'I'm told they even know the changed pitch a ball makes as it's about to drop.'

Column pushers improve their winning chances significantly, which is why dealers shouldn't delay their call for 'no more bets'. It can also cause police evidential problems because a suspect will claim he never heard the call or the call came late. Column pushing is sometimes worked as a two-person sting - one to distract the dealer, the other to place a winning chip.

THE TOP HATTER

Usually there are three top hatters working together; Distractor, Mechanic and Claimant. As the ball is about to drop, the Distractor (often a woman) will try to grab the attention of both dealer and table inspector by loudly demanding a late bet and placing her chips. The dealer will perhaps reach across to stop her, so obscuring the inspector's view. In that instant the ball drops and the Mechanic places chips on the winning number.

This scam is more sophisticated than it appears. Say the Mechanic is playing with yellow chips worth £1 ($1.50) and the Claimant is playing with blue chips worth £10 ($15). At some point the Mechanic will have secretly been passed perhaps five blue chips which he holds in his hand underneath two yellows. That's the top hat. As the ball drops he places this mixed pile onto the winning number.

US president Richard Nixon is said to have financed his first political campaigns on his winnings from army poker sessions. He apparently played a percentage game but, as Watergate later proved, he wasn't a great bluffer.

'If the dealer spots it he might say, "Sorry, sir, that's a late bet,"' says Bhangoo, 'but all he's actually seen is the guy with yellow chips placing a bet. He'll return the chips but only the *yellow* chips. The blues stay in place for the Claimant to take the winnings. In this case that's £50 ($75) at 35-1 and a total of £1,750 ($2,625). Good money for a few seconds' work.

'These people are very, very good. They are so quick and of course they practise for hours before they go to work. I know of one case where someone tried to stack 15 chips on a winning number. It makes you wonder how many times he'd succeeded with fewer chips to even attempt that.'

CARD SHARPS

If you want to cheat the house at cards you have two basic strategies and a third that is so audacious as to be beyond most people. The first pits you against the casino. Typically you'll influence play by marking a pack, swapping cards with accomplices, sneaking glances at other cards using a mirror (known as 'glim working') or concealing cards in a metal contraption under your jacket (sometimes called 'breastworks'). In a big, camera-laden casino with professional supervisors this is all high-risk stuff, though skilled operators can and do get away with it.

Bhangoo recalls one particular prosecution of a casino stud poker player. The cheat had grown his right thumb nail long, cut the corner off a razor blade, superglued it and then painted the nail to make the bond stronger. He used the razor to mark the cards and marked nearly all of them. However, because the scam took too long, the casino spotted what was happening.

In the next strategy the house is on your side, courtesy of a bent dealer:

Casinos are petrified of crooked staff, and rightfully so. We had one case where the dealer was passing cash chips to a player who hadn't even placed a bet. The inspector didn't spot it – inspectors usually have to watch two tables at once – and it was another player who got suspicious.

The casino checked back through its TV security tapes, which are kept for nine or ten days before being re-used. They discovered that in those few days the dealer had passed over something just short of £20,000. Some people say, 'Oh, the casino can afford it.' But that's not the point. If you were to steal the same amount from a Post Office or Marks & Spencer everyone would accept it as serious crime. Why should casinos have any less protection under the law?

Recently we arrested a dealer with an elastic bandage on his wrist. He was stuffing it full of cash chips and had about £1,600 worth on him when he was caught. Casinos can keep track of how many cash chips are in circulation. They know players sometimes take them home but on this table there were always a lot missing on the days this particular dealer was working. The suggestion was that he'd taken £100,000.

Dealers can try to mark the packs they use, perhaps by trimming and sizing high-value cards along the long side (called high belly stripping). In a big casino this is almost impossible because new packs are used every day and shredded when the tables close. More likely, a skilled dealer will use false shuffles to deal his accomplices top cards.

According to media reports crooked staff are taking millions of pounds out of British casino profits. An article in the *Observer* (17 September 2000) told how Napoleon's in London's Leicester Square had lost more than £80,000 ($120,000) during a scam worked by three players and a croupier linked to the 14K Triads, a Chinese criminal gang.

'Collusion is absolutely rife across the industry,' a former Napoleon's croupier told the paper, 'but it's swept under the carpet because casinos don't want the publicity. There are people working as croupiers who have card skills that would put professional magicians to shame. They don't advertise their abilities because they know they would be treated with suspicion. But they can appear to shuffle a deck of cards without changing them at all. That's the key.'

This source claimed the 14K sting targeted one of the club's three punto banco tables. Punto banco – otherwise known as baccarat – is a simple game with a very slender house edge – just over 1 per cent. It's a straight head-to-head contest between one player (the punto) and the bank (banco), although observers can bet on either hand. The aim is to back the hand that achieves a total closest to nine. If the total rises above nine you subtract ten.

Each player is dealt two cards face up. If either punto or banco is dealt a 'natural' eight or nine it wins. Otherwise punto has to stand on a total of six or seven and draw a third card between nought and five. Banco stands or draws as appropriate and all bets are settled. In British casinos a tie leaves all stakes on the table for the next hand. Crucially, for the 14K gang, punto banco is played with six or eight decks shuffled into a shoe. Players are also allowed to make notes on the order in which cards emerge.

At Napoleon's, once the eighth deck had been played the crooked dealer would apparently shuffle the cards but leave a pre-agreed section untouched. His accomplices would play normally until, from their notes, they knew that the unshuffled sequence was in play. At this point the size of their bets would dramatically increase together with their winnings.

Casino inspectors are trained to spot unusual betting patterns but with three players in the conspiracy this must have been difficult. Large variations in punto banco bets are not uncommon and the Triad team kept total winnings below a few thousand pounds per night. The bent dealer also tried to ensure the unshuffled cards appeared during his break or while he worked at other tables.

The scam ended only because the dealer wanted to leave and was ordered by the gang to find a malleable replacement. Although he obliged, the new recruit immediately briefed his bosses on what was happening.

'Once you have customers and staff working together it is extremely difficult to detect and combat it – especially if they're not greedy,' said Kevin Hopley, a director at Napoleon's. 'In this particular case we were unable to ascertain whether a fraud had actually taken place. All we had was evidence of an approach to a member of staff by another croupier.'

A few months before the *Observer* story a similar baccarat scam was smashed at the Claridge Casino Hotel, Atlantic City, by New Jersey detectives working with the state's Division of Gaming Enforcement. This time 13 men and women, mostly of Vietnamese descent, won more than $100,000 (£66,600) in just two hours' play. Again, they needed the help of a crooked dealer and a false shuffle. Two of the gang played first, noting the order of cards before leaving to pass that information on to their co-conspirators. Soon afterwards, nine new players appeared and began to bet big. All were arrested at the table by the DGE along with the dealer and a Mr Big, who controlled the operation.

Marking cards is obviously risky and difficult in a casino. But what if the cards are marked before they get to the casino; before the deck seal has even been broken? That's the third strategy.

In 1999 the owners of Caesars in Johannesburg were troubled. South African casinos were used to making an overall return of 17 per cent on bets and yet across the country that figure had dropped as low as 14 per cent. Some 'experts' imagined it was because South African card players were becoming 'better gamblers'. On the evidence they offered, it could just as easily have been a conspiracy by the Three Bears. Yet *something* had to explain the fall.

When Caesars' blackjack profits plummeted by 1 million rand (£100,000) inside three weeks the casino's exasperated chief executive, Ernie Joubert, ordered all croupiers and inspectors to report suspicious betting patterns. Security cameras began picking up 'irregular and irrational' play by at least four men who always sat in similar positions with a good view of the croupier's cards. They seemed to know exactly when to bet big. In fact, the croupier – who, as house player, was their opponent – might as well have dealt his own cards face up.

In May 1999 Caesars reported that almost every blackjack deck in its casino had been marked. It emerged that a syndicate had bribed or threatened a worker at Protea, the country's only playing card manufacturer, to print a tiny flaw in the pattern of every high-value card. An employee was arrested and police revealed they had four other suspects. Not the least of their problems was a view expressed by legal experts that cheating at cards might not be a criminal offence in South Africa.

Joubert estimated that the syndicate had made 50 million rand (£5 million) from casinos across the country – arguably the most audacious gambling fraud of recent years. 'It's so good, so clever and so subtle, only a skilled or trained eye can see it,' he told reporters. The only reason we caught them was because they became a bit too greedy and took too much too fast.'

CARD COUNTERS

Casinos are the only trading companies that make money by beating their clients at games of chance. If the client becomes so adept that he tilts the odds in his favour through card counting, most gamblers will raise a cheer. Sadly, all casinos will kick the player out.

Counting cards – memorizing those already played – is not easy to master but at blackjack it is a lethal weapon against the house. Blackjack tables do not return cards to the pack after each deal (because it wastes time) and for various procedural reasons there are occasions where the value of the undealt cards will favour the player over the house. Card counters can work this out and that's when they bet big. Sometimes it'll give them a 2 per cent edge.

Naturally, casinos stop at nothing to foil them. Typical precautions include distributing photo mugshots of known exponents, face-recognition computer technology, embedded scanners on tables that can identify the system a player is using, shuffling between every few hands, lowering maximum stakes without warning, preventing a gambler playing multiple hands – even encouraging staff to spill drinks on the counter to unsettle him.

If a counter is identified during a game the casino will usually refuse to pay. (If you think this is unfair, bear in mind that in Nevada you can be legally excluded simply for being too lucky.) However occasionally judges will side with the counter, as did the Nevada Supreme Court in the Richard Chen ruling delivered on 9 March 2000. Chen, a known counter, had used a fictitious Burma passport to obtain $44,000 (£29,300) in chips from the Monte Carlo Casino, Las Vegas. By the time he'd pushed his winnings above $40,000 (£26,000), the casino smelled a rat and stopped the game. They refused to pay and were backed by both the Nevada Gaming Control Board and a district judge.

However the state's Supreme Court decided he'd done nothing wrong. The demand for a passport was a government anti money-laundering requirement, nothing to do with card counting. Chen had committed no crime and he was duly paid off.

'Casinos have a buzz-word for counting,' says Casino Creations' Vic Taucer. 'They call it "advantage play". It's not cheating but it's every bit as dangerous to them and the only difference in their response comes in the way the individual is treated. The cheat gets prosecuted; the counter is invited to leave.

'As a dealer I've thrown out hundreds of them over the years. Casinos which claim they can spot counters quickly are usually too aggressive. It takes time. You have to monitor their play and take more than one look at them. In a blackjack game you'll keep a suspect under close surveillance for at least a couple of hours and assess the strategy he's using based on the disbursement of cards. The only exception is if the counter's strategy is blatant and he's raising and lowering bets with too much voracity.'

SLOTS CHEATS

Slot machine security has come a long way since the days when you could manipulate the pull mechanism to throw up a tasty line of cherries. In Australia the New South Wales government is developing an online computerized monitoring system (CMS) to guard against theft from poker machines. 'Pokies are just tin boxes with motherboards,' one NSW government source told me. 'If you can network computers in an office you can network the pokies. In Queensland and Victoria they already monitor every bet and payout on every machine. There's a failsafe system so that if anyone fiddles with the equipment, bells ring and the whole system shuts down.'

> 'A gambler is someone who plays slot machines. I prefer to own slot machines.''
> Donald Trump

Fair enough. But as any systems engineer will tell you, computer security is vulnerable to penetration by an insider. During the early 1990s the Nevada Gaming Board discovered just *how* vulnerable after it employed Ronald Dale Harris, the world's greatest slots cheat.

On the afternoon of Saturday 14 June 1995 Reid Errol McNeal bought $100 (£66) worth of keno tickets from machines at Bally's Park Place Casino Resort in Atlantic City. He needed to pick eight correct numbers and, sure enough, the winning ticket he presented had all eight, a 230,000-1 chance. The $100,000 (£66,600) jackpot prize was the largest ever won at keno in Atlantic City and yet McNeal seemed pushed to even raise a smile. He had no ID and he wanted his money in cash. As one executive later put it 'he didn't pass the smell test'.

New Jersey law demands that any win over $35,000 (£23,000) is verified by the state gaming division and so officials backed by a couple of state troopers took McNeal back to his hotel room to make further inquiries. There they found his friend Ron Harris. At this point the cops were more curious than suspicious and they left Harris alone while McNeal accompanied them back to the reception desk. There he admitted his friend was an employee of the Nevada Gaming Control Board.

By the time the investigators returned to the bedroom, Harris had scarpered. Troopers searched the room and discovered computer equipment, chips, notes, and books describing how to beat a keno game. McNeal was arrested on the spot and later agreed to testify against Harris in exchange for immunity from prosecution. Harris was picked up as he arrived back at Las Vegas airport.

Police believe he used his job at Nevada's GCB to steal a confidential source code that allowed his laptop computer to synchronize with random number generators inside keno and poker machines. He then downloaded and duplicated the calculations they made, successfully predicting results in advance. In a trial run during December 1994, he and McNeal won $10,000 (£6,600) from a Las Vegas keno machine inside five minutes.

Understandably, Nevada gaming enforcement officers decided to take a close look at Harris's work. It involved testing slot machines to ensure they contained only GCB-approved computer EPROM (erasable programmable read only memory) chips, used to control payout percentages. Harris was found to have erased and re-programmed EPROMs in three casinos so that machines followed a 'gaff' or cheating instruction. When coins were inserted in a certain sequence – ie 3 + 2 + 2 + 1 + 3 + 5 – the maximum jackpot was paid. More than 30 machines were doctored in this way.

On 9 January 1998 Harris was sentenced to seven years by a Nevada District Court on racketeering charges. Afterwards the state's Attorney General, Frankie Sue Del Papa, described the investigation as a turning point in the fight against hi-tech crime. 'This has been an extremely complicated, multi-faceted case involving highly complex computer technology and sophisticated gaming cheating techniques,' he said. 'Perhaps, more than any other single event, the Harris case illustrated to law enforcement, as well as to the corporate community, how vulnerable we are in Nevada and nationwide.'

PAPER MONEY

Vulnerable is a word synonymous with any organization that relies on a few individuals to handle big financial transactions. This happens on a daily basis in world stock markets and great play is made of the hi-tech security enveloping the system like a mighty, impenetrable shield. Would-be rogue traders risk leaving big electronic footprints all over the shop. Checks and counter-checks are built in to every deal. Didn't help Barings Bank, mind.

The adventures of Nick Leeson, general manager at Barings Futures Singapore, perfectly illustrate the dangers of spread betting and loss chasing. In 1993, 25-year-old Leeson was a star dealer for the investment bank, posting a £10 million ($15 million) profit for it and scooping a £130,000 ($195,000) bonus on top of his £50,000 ($75,000) salary. No one questioned his performance. He seemed to have a natural knack for dealing in derivatives, a newish market poorly understood by the Old Boy Brigade at Barings.

Leeson's expertise lay in futures contracts – effectively a promise to buy stock at an agreed price on a future date in the belief that by then it will have risen higher and turned an instant profit. The process also works in reverse; selling an advance position in the hope of a fall. Put simply Leeson was betting on the future direction of the Nikkei, the Japanese stock market. And losing.

He concealed his losses in a special ledger called 88888. Leeson had total control of this account because, in a cutbacks exercise, Barings let him work both as front-of-house trader and backroom settlements manager. He kept up the charade for two years but by December 1994 the red numbers in 88888 were growing bigger by the day.

Leeson staked big futures bets on the Nikkei bouncing at the start of 1995. It didn't and Japan's fragile economy continued to falter. When the devastating Kobe earthquake struck in January the index plunged 8 per cent. This time Leeson convinced himself that a post-quake rebound was imminent. It never materialized. In a doomed one-man attempt to shift market sentiment he bought more than 20,000 futures contracts each worth around £120,000 ($180,000). Now he was acting like the parody of an obsessed sports fan convinced that after three defeats his team just *had* to win the next game.

Finally, on 23 February 1995, his nerve broke. He fled with his wife and was arrested during a flight stopover in Germany. By now Barings' losses totalled more than £800 million ($1.2 billion) and the hapless bank was toast. It was later sold for £1 to Dutch bankers ING and Leeson's bosses either resigned or were sacked. It emerged that they had wired him £650 million ($975 million) to continue trading even after the SIMEX (the Singapore International Monetary Exchange) warned about his dealings. Leeson himself was sentenced in Singapore to six and a half years for fraud.

We can't leave the financial markets without a word on the biggest bet of all time, the £10 billion ($15 billion) punt by Hungarian-born financier George Soros that led to 'Black Wednesday' and a meltdown of share values around the world.

In 1992 Soros staked this money – one and a half times the value of all his funds – on buying German marks. He believed sterling had entered the European Exchange Rate Mechanism at a grossly over-valued level and dismissed the repeated assertions of then-British Prime Minister John Major and his Chancellor, Norman Lamont, that the Bank of England would defend sterling's value. Britain, Lamont insisted, would never leave the ERM. As Soros put it, 'Those words did not carry conviction.'

Major and Lamont spent £6 billion ($9 billion) in a futile attempt to shore up the pound. In the process they discovered that no government – not British, German nor even American – can ever hope to win a financial war with the markets. Once word got out that Soros was betting against sterling the big US currency traders joined the party and sold it themselves. On 16 September 1992 Lamont announced that Britain had suspended membership of the ERM – a move that effectively devalued the pound. At that point Soros converted his marks back to sterling and pocketed a £650 million ($975 million) profit. Soon after this he announced he'd donated £250 million ($375 million) to various worthy causes in eastern Europe.

Later, an ITN interviewer questioned him about Black Wednesday. Did he realize that it had cost every man woman and child in Britain £12 to pay off his bet? 'I really think that every citizen of Great Britain should have contributed £12 to the transformation of eastern Europe,' Soros replied. 'I'm happy to deliver that aid.'

It all brings to mind that wonderful quote from Sir Ernest Cassel, private banker to King Edward VII. 'When I was young,' he said, 'people called me a gambler. As the scale of my operations increased I became known as a speculator. Now I am called a banker. But I have been doing the same thing all the time.'

CLEANING MONEY

Laundering money – that is exchanging traceable notes obtained from criminal activity for 'clean' ones in general circulation – is not as easy as it sounds in a UK casino. You might walk in with £50,000 ($75,000) in stolen dosh, lodge it with the cashier and plan to walk away with a different wad after playing for a few days. What you'll get back are the very same notes you handed in. In Britain, a casino is duty-bound to inform police of suspicious activity but that doesn't mean they report everyone with a £50,000 ($75,000) wedge. Some players habitually carry this kind of cash.

In the US there are even more stringent safeguards. Legislations such as the 1970 Bank Secrecy Act and the 2001 Patriot Act require casinos to report any suspicious monetary or currency exchange. Since March 2003 they also have to file SARs (an unfortunate acronym standing for Suspicious Activity Report) in which the casino must record any unusual transaction above $5,000 (£3,300) with possible links to crime. Casinos are not allowed to tell patrons that they're named in SARs.

It's not quite like this in Monaco, that European mecca of casino culture that Somerset Maugham famously described as 'a sunny place for shady people'. In 2000 a French parliamentary commission produced a report that claimed, 'The Principality has chosen fiscal and commercial legislation and a method of judicial working that does not meet European or international norms.' This is diplomatic parlance for: 'In Monaco your government is dodgy and your entire system is built on corruption and money laundering.' But not even French politicians can actually say that. The report went on specifically to attack the state-owned casino that, it said, operated 'without respect for international standards.'

In 2001 another Paris-based organization, the Financial Action Task Force (FATF), reported its concerns about flaky Internet casinos. As the body co-ordinating international efforts to fight money laundering, it claimed to have evidence of at least three virtual gambling scams that spanned the globe. One of these was a Caribbean e-casino run by a company laundering the proceeds of crime in Europe. Money flows were traced to a bureau de change whose owner had been convicted of breaking gaming regulations. Another shadowy figure in the network had allegedly held up a bank.

The FATF quoted a second example in which $178 million (£120 million) in 'dirty' money had been laundered through a sports touting service that claimed to collect inside information on sports events to sell to subscribers. The task force said it was common for criminals to operate websites promoting fictional gambling companies, using names similar to genuine ones. This allowed them to exploit confusion and mask money-laundering activities.

BASKET CASES

Fixing games is nothing new in America. Ever since 'point-shaving' (taking bribes to deliberately reduce a score) first joined the lexicon of basketball fans in the early 1930s it has dogged college and professional sporting fixtures. In 1945 five Brooklyn College players admitted they were planning to rig a game with Akron University. Four years later a co-captain at George Washington University revealed that four gamblers had attempted to bribe him and during the same season Manhattan College's co-captains were caught offering a bung to one of their own players.

In 1951 the shit and the fan collided with a vengeance as 35 players and former players from campuses such as City College of New York, Long Island University, Toledo, Bradley, New York University and Kentucky confessed to fixing games. The trend got so bad that in 1961 more than 50 players from 27 colleges were found to have fixed games across 22 states.

If it was only college kids betting on each other's teams, point-shaving might not be quite so hard to combat. Unfortunately Mafia types moved in. The Boston College scandal of 1978 resulted in prosecutions against six people, two of whom were linked to a major theft at Kennedy Airport that year. Later another shadowy figure, Sam Perry – also known as 'Richie the Fixer' – was convicted of perpetrating the Boston basketball affair.

Perry, closely connected to the Luchese organized crime family, also ran a nice line in racetrack scams as New York state police discovered in the 1973 Superfecta harness racing scandal. Perry realised that covering every winning combination in an eight-horse race would cost $5,040 (£3,360) for a payoff of around $3,000 (£2,000). But if he bribed three of the drivers to pull back or get boxed in he could back all the remaining horses for an outlay of just $1,089 (£726), a profit of almost $2,000 (£1,300) per set of tickets.

The National Collegiate Athletic Association (NCAA) recognizes that point-shaving in basketball or American Football is now rare. However it continues to push for a total ban on sports betting, currently legal only in Nevada. This position is derided by the gaming industry, which persuasively points out that, in 2000, $2.3 billion (£1.5 billion) was legally waged on Nevada's sports books. In contrast the National Gambling Impact Study Commission estimated that Americans *illegally* staked an annual total of $380 billion (£253 billion) on sport through the Internet and unofficial bar-room or college bookies. It is hard to see how banning that 1 per cent of legal sports betting is going to magically reduce the 99 per cent that is illegal.

INTERNATIONAL BUNGERS

For many years sports administrators around the world stared loftily down at America and tut-tutted at all that corruption. But cozy complacency is never a good idea and in the 1990s these same officials were forced to wake up and smell the coffee. In two of the world's biggest sports, match fixing emerged as a pandemic parasite. To the disbelief of millions, one of the household names implicated was the UK's Liverpool FC star goalkeeper Bruce Grobbelaar – regarded as unpredictable but brilliant. Another was Hansie Cronje, the South African cricket captain accorded almost god-like status in his country. Both men, it was alleged, took money from bookmakers to influence the course of matches.

The crux of the Grobbelaar case was that he had taken cash payments of up to £40,000 ($60,000) to fix certain English league matches. The allegations, made by *The Sun* newspaper, led to a criminal trial in August 1997 after which Grobbelaar and fellow soccer players John Fashanu and Hans Segers were all cleared of a conspiracy to throw games. A fourth defendant, Malaysian businessman Heng Suan Lim, was also acquitted.

This had been the men's second trial on a range of charges linked to a betting syndicate in Malaysia and Indonesia which, the prosecution alleged, made complex wagers on winning margins and aggregate scores. The first collapsed six months earlier when the jury failed to reach a verdict.

One of the matches highlighted was Newcastle United's 3–0 home win over Liverpool in November 1993 in which Grobbelaar was supposedly paid to fix the match at that score. Winchester Crown Court was treated to the bizarre spectacle of former England international goalkeepers Bob Wilson and Gordon Banks giving opinions as to whether Grobbelaar let in these and other goals on purpose. They concluded there was no evidence that any of the defendants had thrown games. Even so, soccer fans across the country began wondering whether their team's goalie was taking a bung. You can probably imagine the pub talk.

After the acquittal, Grobbelaar sued *The Sun* for libel and in 1999 won £85,000 ($127,500) damages from a jury. The newspaper appealed, the Court of Appeal overturned the original jury's verdict as 'perverse' and awarded full costs of £1.2 million ($1.8 million) against Grobbelaar. He then appealed to Britain's highest court, the House of Lords, which by a 4–1 majority reinstated the verdict but cut the costs to a nominal £1.

The senior judge, Lord Bingham, summed up legal disagreement over the 'sting' of the libel. The newspaper had insisted it should win if it proved Grobbelaar had taken bribes to fix matches. Whether or not he *actually* fixed them mattered little. The judge inferred that the original jury accepted Grobbelaar's view that there was no proof of him deliberately letting in goals. However Lord Bingham was acidly clear about the goalkeeper's conduct. 'It would be an affront to justice,' he said, 'if a court of law were to award substantial damages to a man shown to have acted in such flagrant breach of his legal and moral obligations.'

The furore over the case sparked the usual flurry of newspaper investigations into soccer corruption. The *Sunday Telegraph* told how 'match fixing across southeast Asia has turned the national leagues in Malaysia, Thailand and Indonesia into joke tournaments'. According to the paper, soccer bunging had become a £350 million ($525 million) industry, even though most forms of gambling were banned in predominantly Muslim

Malaysia. The authorities were said to adopt a relaxed attitude to underground bookies operating from cafés, restaurants and laundries.

The article also quoted a leading Malaysian sports writer, Johnson Fernandez, whose investigations for the *Malay Mail* revealed that up to £125,000 ($187,500) would be wagered on big games. From this, £25,000 ($37,500) would be spent by bookmakers in an attempt to fix the result. 'The usual *modus operandi*,' said Fernandez, 'is to approach one player, often the goalkeeper, and leave him to sort everything out with his team-mates.' Fernandez claimed to know of several British players who'd been bribed (though he didn't identify them) and quoted specific games between Liverpool and QPR, Arsenal and Sheffield Wednesday, and Aston Villa and Manchester United in which match fixing had been attempted.

> In 1999 the Massachusetts state auditor published a survery of 182 lottery claimants revealing that winnings of $2.2 million (£1.5 million) had been claimed using invalid social security numbers, including those of dead people. The audit attributed this to tax evasion and other fraud.

A further complication is the betting culture that pervades British professional football (see 'Health', p136). Under Football Association rules, players are not supposed to bet on any game in any way other than through authorized football pools. However Graham Sharpe of UK bookmakers William Hill told the *Telegraph* that players were regular customers who used inside knowledge to full effect. 'We see it as legitimate gamesmanship,' he said. 'If a team changes their penalty taker and we don't know about it then they may be getting 25-1 or 33-1 about what is really a 10-1 shot.'

Perhaps he was thinking of a certain case in 1992 when Colchester United's players pulled off an entirely legal betting sting. They backed defender Martin Granger as their team's first scorer at 20-1, knowing that he'd just been made penalty taker by player manager Roy McDonough, the usual spot-kick specialist. Sure enough, Colchester got a penalty, Granger slotted it home and his team-mates celebrated a collective win of £4,000 ($6,000). This despite losing their cup match 2-1 to Northampton Town.

A final word on football betting. Don't make the mistake one Scottish punter made in 1992 when he altered his pools coupon in an attempt to convince Ladbrokes he'd correctly predicted the results of all 61 Boxing Day football league matches. His stake was a mere 50p and Ladbrokes calculated that if he was right, they owed him £3,826 billion ($5,739 billion), ten times Britain's gross national product and 65 times the nation's annual tax revenue. The punter pleaded guilty to forgery with intent to deceive.

HOWZAT!

Football fixing is one thing. With all those hooligans, gambling-mad players and transfer bungs what do you expect! But *cricket*? Surely not the sport of gentleman where the thwack of leather on willow conjures up images of warm beer, cucumber sandwiches, the lengthening shadows of a still summer's evening, that deathly hush as the last man strides to the wicket?

Unfortunately, cricket is indeed bent. Not all cricketers of course but enough to give the sport a serious headache as it comes to terms with the magnitude of the Hansie Cronje scandal. Cricket's problem lies mainly with Indian and Pakistani bookmakers trading in countries where the game is a national obsession. If the Indian test side is playing live, the anticipated TV audience will be around 300 million, or 50 million more than the entire resident population of the United States. These are fans who enjoy a bet and their total stakes can make or break bookmakers.

Cricket gambling in southern Asia is presently controlled by two Mafia syndicates, one in Pakistan and the other based in Bombay. For some reason Sharad Shetty, a senior figure in the Pakistan operation, was found shot dead in Dubai on 19 January 2003 during the run-up to the cricket World Cup. Many in the sub-continent believe he was preparing the ground for a betting coup in which matches would not so much be thrown as manipulated.

In cricket, this is surprisingly easy to achieve. Perhaps it's because players can be persuaded that, if matches are 'dead' (ie their team is already through a qualifying group) or victory is assured then no one is being cheated. No one, that is, except the humble punter. The other comforting fact is that it's all so effortless.

Say you're an in-form batsman. You're told to get yourself out after reaching 50, when punters will be scrabbling to back you for a century.

Perhaps you're a fast bowler who could help make 'extras' the highest score in an innings by bowling a few wides and no-balls. And if you're an umpire maybe you could uphold precisely two leg before wicket appeals during the innings.

It was an investigation by Indian police and tax officials that finally laid bare Hansie Cronje's duplicity. Phone taps suggested he was being bribed to fix games and a look at his financial affairs later revealed he held more than 70 Cayman Islands bank accounts. At first, the South African captain denied everything. 'I am telling you 110 per cent,' he told a press conference in April 2000, 'I am not guilty.'

Three days later, at three in the morning, Cronje broke down and confessed to his pastor, Ray MacAuley. Later that day a carefully worded press statement began; 'I have not been entirely honest.' A few months later he admitted to the King Commission on cricket corruption in South Africa that he had accepted $130,000 (£86,700) from bookies for influencing matches and individual performances within them. He said he had 'allowed Satan and the world to dictate terms' and confessed to an 'unfortunate love of money', which he compared to drug and alcohol addiction. 'The moment I took my eyes off Jesus,' he added, 'my whole world turned dark.'

In his testimony Cronje told how he had offered bribes of $15,000 (£10,000) apiece to two players – Herschelle Gibbs and Henry Williams – to play below par in a one-day game against India. He also agreed he'd received £5,000 ($7,500) and a leather jacket from a South African bookmaker to contrive a result from a test match between England and South Africa in January 2000. But these admissions were straws in the wind. Everybody – especially the King Commission – believed his 'confession' was far from complete given the enormity of the bribes being made.

According to the *Sunday Telegraph* Indian police knew that several cricketers were accepting $50,000 (£33,300) per month to 'supply information' to bookmakers and that the Indian Mafia was paying out £3 million ($4.5 million) per month to influence test matches and one-day internationals. This sounds a lot until you realize that, according to the International Cricket Council, more than $250 million (£167 million) is gambled on the average one-dayer.

It's unlikely we'll ever know the full truth because in June 2002 Hansie Cronje died in a plane crash in the Outeniqua mountains, aged just 32.

TURF TALES

There's nothing like a good, meaty horseracing scandal. The novelist Dick Francis knew this well, selling millions of books on the strength of plots thickened with dodgy horsey types bearing hypodermic needles. But doping horses is more than the stuff of fiction. Here's a few of the best-known scams.

THE RINGER

This is a classic scam in which an owner or trainer surreptitiously swaps a horse with poor form (and therefore long odds) for one that is a class act. Obviously, the two beasts have to be lookalikes.

The best-known example in Britain is that of Flockton Grey, which romped home by 20 lengths during a race at Leicester in 1982, despite being a 10-1 outside chance. In fact it wasn't Flockton Grey at all but Good Hand, a rather more experienced and fleet-footed three-year-old. Owner Ken Richardson was later 'warned off' (ie banned from the racing industry) for 25 years by the Jockey Club. Punters, knowingly or not, netted £36,000 ($54,000) from the result.

DOPING

In greyhound racing there are, I'm told, 101 ways to affect a dog's performance. These range from feeding it a couple of Mars bars five minutes before a race (to make it go slower) or easing a peeled chilli up its bottom (wouldn't *you* run quicker?). But a racehorse is trickier. For one thing, the animal is much bigger and personally you wouldn't catch me shoving a green chilli up its arse. No, with horses, drugs are the thing.

Currently in British racing there are two particular substances in the spotlight. One is EPO, otherwise known as erythropoietin, which supposedly works by stimulating natural hormones to produce more red blood cells. More red cells mean more oxygen delivered to muscles and greater stamina.

Some vets are unconvinced that EPO works in any meaningful way on a racehorse. Even so the Jockey Club is taking seriously reports of its use.

In February 2002 investigators raided five leading National Hunt stables to take blood samples from 408 horses, roughly 8 per cent of all those registered nationwide. All were negative. Some cynics suggested the testing programme was completed with indecent haste and that both blood and urine samples should have been taken (as is the case with athletes). Yet these raids suggest racing is not quite so tainted as some would have you believe.

The second drug is ACP, or acetylpromazine. This is the fast-acting sedative used by Dermot 'Needle Man' Browne who embarked on a seven-week doping spree in August and September 1990. Browne's syringe nobbled favourites such as Bravefoot (11-8) at Doncaster, Hatell (11-8) at Glorious Goodwood, and Argentum, a runner in Group 1 race the Nunthorpe Stakes. In November 2002 Browne was finally found guilty by the Jockey Club and warned off until 2022. It seems his penalty reflected his assistance in supplying the names of other fixers.

Browne had already named the Mr Big behind his doping activities as Brian Wright, a suspected drug smuggler and currently a fugitive from justice. As he left Jockey Club headquarters he admitted that some of the 'wrong 'uns' were still in racing. 'They're the ones I'd like to see out of it as well,' he said. 'Why don't they come out and admit what they've done? I've left information here and I'm sure they're going to take it on.'

As far as ACP is concerned the guilty men are more likely to be trainers than jockeys. For one thing the drug needs to be administered at least 30 minutes before a race. Jockeys usually see their mount only 10 minutes beforehand, by which time they're on full public view. Secondly, who wants to ride a doped horse? 'As a jockey,' wrote Marcus Armytage in the *Daily Telegraph* (28 January 1998) 'I wouldn't knowingly want to ride a sedated horse in a race any more than I'd like to peer over Beachy Head during a northerly gale.'

NON-TRIERS
In the same piece Armytage outlined the simpler, safer ways for a bent jockey to operate. 'There are many ways a jockey can stop a horse winning other than risking his reputation by getting involved with doping,' he wrote. 'Riding a tactically injudicious race; making too much use of the

horse during the early stages; not riding a forceful finish; not helping the horse at an obstacle; taking it wide for the better ground, the possibilities are endless.'

To these you can add 'non-triers', jockeys who deliberately hold a horse back despite its form or handicap. Broadcaster John McCririck says the Jockey Club has been having a purge on this practice. 'The jockey's typical response is that his horse is "gurgling", or making a funny noise,' McCririck told me. 'This is supposed to be an indication that the horse is in trouble though just recently there seems to have been an awful lot of it about. I've never known such a gurgling outbreak in all my life.

'Race fixing is much less prevalent in Britain nowadays but strange things still go on in small fields. There's a simple solution, which is to ensure that no race begins with fewer than six runners. This makes it harder to fix the result because more people have to be in on the scam. I know some owners and trainers will object and it may be difficult for the smaller race meetings. But it would tackle the problem.'

McCririck believes media race-nobbling exposés have been hugely damaging to an industry that, in the past, has been too complacent. 'That said, we at least do ask questions in this country,' he said. 'In America, if there's a dodgy-looking result no one ever says a word. They just get on with the next race.'

BETTING COUPS

Up to a point, Mac. In America one or two eyebrows *were* raised following the October 2002 Breeders' Cup at Arlington Park, Illinois, when Derrick Davis of Baltimore apparently defied the odds to produce a $3 million (£2 million) winning prediction. This scam – dubbed the Pick Six Scandal – was wonderfully simple. It worked because Davis's accomplice and former Drexel University fraternity brother Chris Harn was an employee of Autotote, America's largest processor of racehorse betting. Harn helped Davis to select the first four horses – not difficult seeing as they'd already won.

Once again, this scam depended on a computer security flaw. The Breeders' Cup Pick Six required punters to predict the winners of all six races on the card and stake their money before the first was run. Bets placed at Off-Track-Betting (OTB) shops across the country were logged centrally with Autotote and the total sum wired to Arlington Park to be combined with on-track wagers. The aim of this is to increase the size of the overall pool up for grabs under the tote system.

> 'The Jockey Club is concerned about the vulnerability of horseracing to criminal behaviour and other undesirable activity as a consequence of betting.' Submission to the UK Gambling Review Body by the Jockey Club, 2002

Harn discovered that although the total amount was wired through, individual bets were not sent to the track until after the first four races had been run. The computer systems designers were obviously concerned about network capacity and wanted to avoid the possible gridlock of all individual Pick Six bets being transmitted simultaneously.

Davis's $12 (£8) stake, placed through a telephone account with Catskill's of New York, selected specific winners for the first four races and combined them with every possible winning combination for the final two. When Harn got hold of his electronic bet it was a relatively simple task to alter the first four selections to feature the winners – Domedriver (26-1), Orientate (2.7-1), Starine (13.2-1) and Vindication (4.1-1). Both Harn and Davis pleaded guilty and received prison terms of between two and four years.

NET LOSSES

The Pick Six was a clear and direct fraud. In contrast the advent of Internet betting exchanges has produced a much subtler manipulation, one almost impossible to detect. As a professional tipster, Steve Lewis Hamilton is not happy about it:

> If corruption becomes rife it's no good to me. What's the point in doing all your form work if you're betting on a dodgy race? I can usually second guess what trainers are doing with their horses but amateur punters in the shop don't have that knowledge. The bigger meetings and big races are no problem. The horses are there to win. The problem lies with the smaller, midweek meetings.

The betting exchanges have opened new doors to corruption. In the past if you wanted to lay a horse you didn't think would win it was all very convoluted. The bookmaker might feel there wasn't enough in it for him and wouldn't accept. Nowadays if I own a horse, and I know it's missed some work, I can lay it and nobody will know any different. There's no trace. There's nothing to stop me ringing up my uncle and asking him to act on my behalf on the exchanges.

I used to own a horse called Physical Force. In February 2002 he was 7-4 favourite at an evening meeting in Wolverhampton. What was to stop me ordering the jockey not to win and then laying that horse on the betting exchanges - offering £2,000 at 9-4. I'd have taken plenty of bets from punters believing they had good-value odds when in fact they had no chance of winning. Nobody would ever have known. In fact I didn't fancy Physical Force and he didn't win. Neither did I lay odds on him.

I've spoken to senior managers at the exchanges about this and they'll tell you the computers can trace every bet. The problem is that with National Hunt racing you're not talking about a lot of money. The jockeys get £100 per ride and the owners are quite happy to make a couple of grand laying odds. It's not like they're laying to lose £100,000 - that would obviously show up.

There's so much business on the exchanges that people are prepared to back any horse in a race. I don't know how this is going to be dealt with. I don't know the solution. All I know is that most owners in jump races want to win. The problem arises when an owner suspects his best hope will finish second or third. That's when he'll tell the jockey to go easy.

Some days you'll see the shows [odds] come through from the course and the shows on the betting exchanges and you know something's going off because there's such a huge discrepancy. There's no big secret about this. Everyone knows it goes on. Racing wants to turn a blind eye because it's easier to ignore than it is to deal with.

If all this boggles your brain, relax. The old reliable con-merchant is still alive and well on Britain's racecourses, even for high-profile events like the Derby. In 1997 punters placed bets with a bookmaker called John Batten who set himself up on the Hill – part of the downs that offers free entry. He flashed his licence at racecourse staff and paid his £75 ($105) fee.

Other bookmakers noticed him but thought little of it. There are a lot of strange faces at the track on Derby Day and although Batten was offering slightly better odds than his rivals there was plenty of business to go round. Only when punters turned up to collect their winnings did the alarm bells sound. Of 'Mr Batten' there was no sign; neither was there any trace of the estimated £40,000 ($60,000) he stuffed into his pockets. It was not lost on racegoers that the Derby winner that day was Benny The Dip, a horse named after a pickpocket in a Damon Runyon story.

BEATING THE ODDS

We end on a story so good that if it wasn't true you'd swear it was an urban myth. Step forward the Hole-In-One-Gang, two former betting officer managers called John Carter and Paul Simmons from Essex.

They teamed up in 1987 as professional gamblers and soon realized that the best odds around were offered against golfers shooting holes-in-one at professional tournaments. While the big bookmakers – William Hill, Ladbrokes and Coral – knew the true odds stood at even money or 6–4, hundreds of smaller bookies hadn't properly investigated the bet. They seemed unaware of improving standards within the game and the vastly increased number of good players on the circuit.

During a trial run the pair got odds as high as 50–1 before staging a 'de luxe' coup against some 4,000 independent betting shops in England and South Wales. They planned this like a military operation, photocopying hundreds of telephone listings and buying street maps of every town and city to achieve the most time-efficient schedule.

In 1991 they together drove 50,000 miles (80,465km), varying and limiting their stakes to avoid suspicion. Carter played the role of a mild-mannered office worker who planned to spend his holidays visiting major tournaments. He started by asking for a small bet then teamed it with doubles, trebles and other accumulators worth more than £10,000 ($15,000) in potential winnings. Simmons was the brash, big-betting punter who carried up to £5,000 ($7,500) in cash and threw in 'mixer' or 'sweetener' bets on soccer and cricket before inquiring about golf odds. Together they staked a total of £30,000 ($45,000).

From the moment the tournament season began, the holes-in-one rolled in. But the big payoff depended heavily on success in five 'banker' tournaments tied in to most of the multiple bets. When Miguel Jimenez obliged at the 155-yard 17th during the European Open at Walton Heath – last of the Big Five – it was worth £3,255 ($4,883) a yard and guaranteed a total payout of £500,000 ($750,000). Most bookmakers honoured the bets. Disgracefully, 11 didn't – presumably relying on the argument that it isn't fair for punters to know the true odds.

Above all else, this story shows the bookmaker is not invincible. If you're patient, meticulous and determined you can choose your sport and leave him crying. Don't forget the Hole-In-One Gang. They proved that successful gambling has nothing to do with luck.

If a bet was ever beautiful, theirs was it.

ADDITIONAL INFO

'The reason he is called Sky is because he goes so high when it comes to betting on any proposition whatever. He will bet all that he has, and nobody can bet any more than that.' - Damon Runyon

As westerners, how much are we prepared to bet? In a world obsessed by status, image and immediacy, gambling is regarded as the quickest and probably only way for most of us to sup at the high table. We're not bothered about dipping into comfortable levels of wealth. To truly live the good life, we want to soak ourselves.

But what is rich? In 2002 one respected British national newspaper editor told his staff that the word 'millionaire' had been banned from copy because it didn't mean much. 'With current house prices almost everyone's a millionaire, aren't they?' he insisted.

Well, no, actually. But his *diktat* raises some interesting questions about perceptions of wealth in the western world. Lottery prizes of £3-4 million ($4.5-6 million) now raise little more than a yawn in newsrooms. Big wins on the horses or in casinos attract few headlines unless the lucky punter is either (a) famous or (b) has won by nefarious means. And have you noticed how all those brash, in-your-face TV cash-prize game shows have died the death? They relied heavily on the hysterical reactions of ecstatic contestants winning the family car. If it happened today the cameras would be lucky to get a jaded smile.

One obvious exception is the TV quiz show *Who Wants To Be A Millionaire?* But the secret of its formula lies not so much in winning a million (very few contestants do) but in the way it presents quiz questions as pure theatre – milking the tension, encouraging audience participation, maximizing light and sound to create a crucible of emotion. Yet the signs are that, even for *Millionaire*, enthusiasm is waning.

In poorer communities, where savings are a luxury and the laws of chance are widely misunderstood, the gambling industry can still get away with trading on wealth dreams. But to woo affluent, free-spending middle-class punters – in other words the people who shore up profit margins – the days are long gone when you could flag up big prizes, sit back and take the money. Gamblers are now wised-up and sophisticated. Why would they take risible odds from Having-A-Laugh Bookmakers Ltd when there's so many places to shop around?

To get us to bet, and bet more, casinos and bookies know they've got to make their product less life-changing and more exciting – betting for fun as much as to win. Online and mobile phone technology is going to drive this process, allowing the chance to bet real time on any event happening anywhere. Casinos will focus more on gambling as a spectacle and a 'night out'; sports betting linked to live TV will be the lifeblood of the 21st-century bookie. The relaxation of gambling laws – an inevitable result of betting freedom on the Internet – will add a new dimension to the world economy.

At least, this is one viewpoint. Another is that society will move the other way; that gambling will be seen as an ever-more corrupting social disease on a par with drinking and smoking. History shows there's nothing new in such paradigms but for anti-gambling lobbyists there has never been a better opportunity to exploit the mass media. Even today, many of us retain a stubborn Protestant ethic, which holds that betting is the devil's work.

Why should this be so? Why should newspapers condemn a highly paid footballer for betting two, three or four million quid if he wants? The issue is surely not how much he spends; it's whether his gambling is a problem. If he stuck this amount into the stock market – a gamble and never let anyone convince you otherwise – then why wouldn't he suffer similar opprobrium? Because, for sure, he wouldn't.

Gambling is full of such contradictions. Whatever the arguments in its favour it unquestionably destroys lives and until we find out how and why, it'll keep giving off that nasty smell my granny so loathed.

Ultimately, scientists hold the key. If they ever pin down the causes of compulsive gambling, and show how to prevent and treat it, then a start can be made on dismantling the myths. In the meantime, all we have is theory. Which brings to mind the wonderful quote from Israel Rosenfield's novel *Freud's Megalomania*: 'The fate of all scientific endeavours is oblivion and...the lucky scientist dies well before the first cracks appear in his edifice.'

For now, if you're going to gamble, the advice remains the same. Be solvent. Be informed. Be careful.

If all else fails, be lucky.

GLOSSARY

Accumulator – a bet in which the return from the first race becomes the stake for the second and so on. Doubles, trebles and yankees are among the most popular

Ante – a stake made before cards are dealt ensuring that each player has 'bought in' to the hand

Ante-post – bets made before the day of a sporting event. The odds may be better but the stake can be lost if, for instance, a horse doesn't race

Bank – the amount provided by a casino to finance one of its gaming tables. Not to be confused with a casino's total working capital

Basic strategy – the best possible playing strategy for a hand dealt from a full, shuffled pack of cards

Bung – another term for a bribe

Call – poker term that means staking enough extra chips to match the last bet

Card counting – memorizing cards already played in order to improve strategy

Carpet-joint – US slang term for an upmarket casino

Chasing – betting to recover losses

Chip – coloured token used in casinos instead of cash

Cognitive behaviour therapy – addiction treatment that teaches addicts to analyze and reform their behaviour

Craps – American casino game usually played with two dice

Dopamine – a pleasure-giving neurotransmitter

Down bet – in spread betting, backing the points score to be below the lower margin set by the bookmaker

Drop – the total number of chips bought at a casino

DSM-IV – a screening system to help determine whether someone is a 'problem gambler'

Edge – the odds advantage enjoyed by a casino or bookmaker

Even money – a bet in which the winnings equal the stake

Folding – to drop out of a hand of cards and lose money already staked

Gaff – a cheating program illegally inserted into a slot machine

Gamblers' fallacy – the false notion that a winning bet becomes more likely after a string of losses

Handicap – a horserace in which the better horses carry saddle weights to give all runners a more equal chance

Keno - lottery-type game, which is popular in America

Lay - to offer odds on an event. To accept a bet

Lay off - reducing payout liability by placing a popular bet with another bookie

Long odds - a horse or competitor considered to have little chance of winning, for example odds of 100-1

Mechanic - term used to describe a professional casino cheat

Nap - a racing tipster's value tip of the day

Neuron - a brain cell that sends electrical messages

Neurotransmitter - chemicals released by brain cells to convey feelings of pleasure, sadness etc

Pathological gambler - a medical term for an addicted or compulsive gambler

Point-shaving - the act of a professional sportsman who deliberately flunks point-scoring (for example, in basketball) in exchange for a bribe

Pokies - Australian slang for slot machines that play virtual poker

Probability theory - a mathematical law governing the occurrence of random events

Problem gambler - the definition of someone whose life has become disrupted through gambling

Proposition bet - a wager not covered by usual rules. A side bet

Raise - a wager that requires other card players to increase their stake in order for them to stay in the game

Re-uptake - the process by which the brain reabsorbs neurotransmitters

Pitch - the spot at which a racetrack bookie plies his trade

Shoe - a device used by a dealer to hold shuffled cards

SOGS - South Oaks Gambling Screen. This questionnaire is used to identify problem gamblers

Stacked - a term used to describe a deck of cards prepared for cheating

Stand - a card player's decision not to draw further cards

Starting price - odds agreed through a consensus of on-track bookies

Synapse - a gap between brain cells in which neurotransmitters operate

Tipster - a professional racing or sports expert who sells tips on likely winners and results

Top hatting - a system of cheating by covertly stacking casino chips.

12-step programme - addiction therapy that focuses on reasserting control through spiritual and practical means

Up-bet - in spread betting, this refers to backing the points score to be above the upper margin set by the bookmaker

Value - in betting parlance, a stake in which the true odds are considered less than those quoted by a bookmaker

ACKNOWLEDGEMENTS

My thanks to the interviewees listed below, all of whom gave up time willingly and in a spirit of sharing knowledge. Any errors or omissions in this book are entirely my responsibility. (Sources have been credited in text wherever possible.)

Andy and Sandra

Inspector Ben Bhangoo, Metropolitan Police Gaming Unit, London

John Delaney, chief executive, Tradesports.com, Dublin

Elizabeth M George, director, North American Training Institute, Duluth, Minnesota

Steve Lewis Hamilton of online tipsters slh.co.uk

John McCririck, broadcaster and journalist, *Channel 4 Racing*

Professor Jan McMillen, director, Centre for Gambling Research, Australian National University, Canberra

Dr Greg Anderson, economist and administrative director at the Centre for Gambling Studies, Salford University, Manchester, England

Dr Howard Shaffer, director, Division on Addictions, Harvard Medical School

Professor Garry Smith, Alberta Gaming Research Institute, Canada

Mark Strahan, webmaster, ukpoker.com

Professor Vic Taucer, head of US company Casino Creations and professor of casino management at the University and Community College, Nevada

And thanks to at least a dozen other people who, for various reasons, prefer to remain anonymous.

INDEX